OBJECT LESSONS

A book series about the hidden lives of ordinary things.

Series Editors:

Ian Bogost and Christopher Schaberg

W0037578

In association with

Program
in Public Scholarship

Washington
University in St.Louis

The Object Lessons series achieves something very close to magic: the books take ordinary—even banal—objects and animate them with a rich history of invention, political struggle, science, and popular mythology. Filled with fascinating details and conveyed in sharp, accessible prose, the books make the everyday world come to life. Be warned: once you've read a few of these, you'll start walking around your house, picking up random objects, and musing aloud: 'I wonder what the story is behind this thing?'"

Steven Johnson, author of *Where Good Ideas Come From* and *How We Got to Now*

Object Lessons describes themselves as 'short, beautiful books,' and to that, I'll say, amen. . . . If you read enough Object Lessons books, you'll fill your head with plenty of trivia to amaze and annoy your friends and loved ones—caution recommended on pontificating on the objects surrounding you. More importantly, though . . . they inspire us to take a second look at parts of the everyday that we've taken for granted. These are not so much lessons about the objects themselves, but opportunities for self-reflection and storytelling. They remind us that we are surrounded by a wondrous world, as long as we care to look."

John Warner, *The Chicago Tribune*

Besides being beautiful little hand-sized objects themselves, showcasing exceptional writing, the wonder of these books is that they exist at all . . . Uniformly excellent, engaging, thought-provoking, and informative."

Jennifer Bort Yacovissi, *Washington Independent Review of Books*

. . . edifying and entertaining . . . perfect for slipping in a pocket and pulling out when life is on hold."

Sarah Murdoch, *Toronto Star*

For my money, Object Lessons is the most consistently interesting nonfiction book series in America."

Megan Volpert, *PopMatters*

Though short, at roughly 25,000 words apiece, these books are anything but slight."

Marina Benjamin, *New Statesman*

[W]itty, thought-provoking, and poetic. . . . These little books are a page-flipper's dream."

John Timpane, *The Philadelphia Inquirer*

The joy of the series, of reading *Remote Control*, *Golf Ball*, *Driver's License*, *Drone*, *Silence*, *Glass*, *Refrigerator*, *Hotel*, and *Waste* (more titles are listed as forthcoming) in quick succession, lies in encountering the various turns through which each of their authors has been put by his or her object. As for Benjamin, so for the authors of the series, the object predominates, sits squarely center stage, directs the action. The object decides the genre, the chronology, and the limits of the study. Accordingly, the author has to take her cue from the *thing* she chose or that chose her. The result is a wonderfully uneven series of books, each one a *thing* unto itself."

Julian Yates, *Los Angeles Review of Books*

The Object Lessons series has a beautifully simple premise. Each book or essay centers on a specific object. This can be mundane or unexpected, humorous or politically timely. Whatever the subject, these descriptions reveal the rich worlds hidden under the surface of things."

Christine Ro, *Book Riot*

. . . a sensibility somewhere between Roland Barthes and Wes Anderson."

Simon Reynolds, author of *Retromania: Pop Culture's Addiction to Its Own Past*

My favourite series of short pop culture books"

Zoomer magazine

Bloomsbury's Object Lessons series never misses"

The Millions

BOOKS IN THE SERIES

Air Conditioning by Hsuan L. Hsu
Alarm by Alice Bennett
Barcode by Jordan Frith
Bicycle by Jonathan Maskit
Bird by Erik Anderson
Blackface by Ayanna Thompson
Blanket by Kara Thompson
Blue Jeans by Carolyn Purnell
Bookshelf by Lydia Pyne
Bread by Scott Cutler Shershow
Bulletproof Vest by Kenneth R. Rosen
Burger by Carol J. Adams
Cell Tower by Steven E. Jones
Cigarette Lighter by Jack Pendarvis
Coffee by Dinah Lenney
Compact Disc by Robert Barry
Doctor by Andrew Bomback
Dust by Michael Marder
Earth by Jeffrey Jerome Cohen and Linda T. Elkins-Tanton
Egg by Nicole Walker
Email by Randy Malamud
Environment by Rolf Halden
Exit by Laura Waddell
Eye Chart by William Germano
Fat by Hanne Blank
Glass by John Garrison
Golf Ball by Harry Brown
Doll Maria Teresa Hart
Driver's License by Meredith Castile
Drone by Adam Rothstein
Fake by Kati Stevens
Football by Mark Yakich
Gin by Shonna Milliken Humphrey
Glitter by Nicole Seymour
Grave Allison C. Meier
Hair by Scott Lowe
Hashtag by Elizabeth Losh
High Heel by Summer Brennan
Hood by Alison Kinney
Hotel by Joanna Walsh
Hyphen by Pardis Mahdavi
Island by Julian Hanna
Jet Lag by Christopher J. Lee
Lawn by Giovanni Aloi
Luggage by Susan Harlan
Magazine by Jeff Jarvis
Magnet by Eva Barbarossa

Mask by Sharrona Pearl
Mushroom by Sara Rich
Newspaper by Maggie Messitt
Ocean by Steve Mentz
Office by Sheila Liming
Oil by Michael Tondre
OK by Michelle McSweeney
Password by Martin Paul Eve
Pencil by Carol Beggy
Perfume by Megan Volpert
Personal Stereo by Rebecca Tuhus-Dubrow
Phone Booth by Ariana Kelly
Pill by Robert Bennett
Political Sign by Tobias Carroll
Potato by Rebecca Earle
Pregnancy Test by Karen Weingarten
Pub by Philip Howell
Questionnaire by Evan Kindley
Recipe by Lynn Z. Bloom
Refrigerator by Jonathan Rees
Remote Control by Caetlin Benson-Allott
Rust by Jean-Michel Rabaté
Saxophone by Mollie Hawkins
Sewer by Jessica Leigh Hester
Scream by Michael J. Seidlinger
Shipping Container by Craig Martin
Shopping Mall by Matthew Newton
Signature by Hunter Dukes
Silence by John Biguenet
Skateboard by Jonathan Russell Clark
Sock by Kim Adrian
Souvenir by Rolf Potts
Snake by Erica Wright
Spacecraft by Timothy Morton
Space Rover by Stewart Lawrence Sinclair
Sticker by Henry Hoke
Stroller by Amanda Parrish Morgan
Swimming Pool by Hsuan L. Hsu
Traffic by Paul Josephson
Tree by Matthew Battles
Trench Coat by Jane Tynan
Tumor by Anna Leahy
TV by Susan Bordo
Veil by Rafia Zakaria
Waste by Brian Thill
Whale Song by Margret Grebowicz
Wine by Meg Bernhard
X-ray by Nicole Lobdell

Saxophone

MOLLIE HAWKINS

BLOOMSBURY ACADEMIC
NEW YORK • LONDON • OXFORD • NEW DELHI • SYDNEY

BLOOMSBURY ACADEMIC
Bloomsbury Publishing Inc
1385 Broadway, New York, NY 10018, USA
50 Bedford Square, London, WC1B 3DP, UK
29 Earlsfort Terrace, Dublin 2, Ireland

BLOOMSBURY, BLOOMSBURY ACADEMIC and the Diana logo are trade-
marks of Bloomsbury Publishing Plc

First published in the United States of America 2025

For legal purposes the Acknowledgements on p. 127 constitute an extension of
this copyright page.

Cover design by Alice Marwick
Cover illustration © Cristiano Siqueira / www.crisvector.com

Bloomsbury Publishing Inc does not have any control over, or responsibility for, any
third-party websites referred to or in this book. All internet addresses given in this
book were correct at the time of going to press. The author and publisher regret
any inconvenience caused if addresses have changed or sites have ceased to exist,
but can accept no responsibility for any such changes.

Whilst every effort has been made to locate copyright holders the publish-
ers would be grateful to hear from any person(s) not here acknowledged.

Library of Congress Cataloging-in-Publication Data

Names: Hawkins, Mollie, author.
Title: Saxophone / Mollie Hawkins.
Description: [1.] | New York: Bloomsbury Academic, 2025. |
Series: Object lessons; vol 95 | Includes index.
Identifiers: LCCN 2024029141 (print) | LCCN 2024029142 (ebook) |
ISBN 9798765114773 (paperback) | ISBN 9798765114780 (ebook) |
ISBN 9798765114797 (pdf)
Subjects: LCSH: Saxophone–History. | Saxophone–Social aspects |
Saxophonists–Anecdotes.
Classification: LCC ML975 .H38 2025 (print) | LCC ML975 (ebook) |
DDC 788.7/19–dc23/eng/20240626
LC record available at https://lccn.loc.gov/2024029141
LC ebook record available at https://lccn.loc.gov/2024029142

ISBN:PB: 979-8-7651-1477-3
ePDF: 979-8-7651-1479-7
eBook: 979-8-7651-1478-0

Series: Object Lessons

Typeset by Deanta Global Publishing Services, Chennai, India
Print and Bound in the United States of America

To find out more about our authors and books visit www.bloomsbury.com
and sign up for our newsletters.

CONTENTS

Prologue 1

PART I: BEFORE IT WAS COOL

1 Dark Origins 7

2 The Sound 25

Sheet Music #1: Raised by a Sax Man 33

3 Everyone is Laughing 39

PART II: ON THE MARGINS

4 Improvisation 47

Sheet Music #2: No More Weddings,

No More Funerals 59

5 Obsession 65

Sheet Music #3: Call and Response 71

6 Seduction 79

Sheet Music #4: Nuisance 85

PART III: **A CULT OF PERSONALITY**

7 Sacred and Profane 91

Sheet Music #5: Pointless Devotion 97

8 Nonconformist 105

9 Influencer 111

Epilogue: Two Horns 123

Acknowledgements 127
Index 131

PROLOGUE

I'm standing at the shuttle stop at the Sacramento airport, waiting for a bus to take me to the rental car garage. It's two weeks before Christmas in 2021, and it's a lot colder than I ever remember it being when I lived there. It's 10:30 p.m. and I did not dress appropriately, so I pull the drawstring of my thin hoodie as tight as it will go and keep the N95 mask sucked to my face for warmth. It wasn't cold in Seattle yet, where I'd just moved for work. *Just* moved, as in, most of my belongings were in boxes, and I didn't have time to find a coat in a sea of cardboard.

That morning I'd booked the only nonstop flight I could find from Seattle to Sacramento, terrified I wouldn't make it there before the Bad Thing happened, and I wasn't thinking about layers, or unpacking, or preparedness. I was thinking about my father. Specifically, hoping he was still alive. I'd been told on the phone that things were bad, his lungs were failing, that Covid was winning, and so fast, my god, and "that's just what happens sometimes."

My first thought was, *How could his lungs be failing? Impossible! He's been playing his saxophone for at least two hours every single day since he was in middle school. That's at least fifty years. Aren't those lungs made of steel at this point? Christ!*

Standing next to me, also waiting for the car rental shuttle, are two older couples. They're giving me side glances—maybe because I'm traveling alone, that I look suspicious in my sweatshirt, the hood pulled so tightly around my masked face that I may as well try to steal their wallets. My eyes are red, and I keep sniffling because I've been ugly crying ugly for hours on a plane, and in the current social standards, sniffling means you're contagious. I think about telling them I'm not sick, I'm just having the worst day of my life, but I don't want to make it awkward. But Covid is awkward. Society is awkward. It's practically illegal to stand too close to anyone, so many pieces of tape marking the X in which we must stand.

Ambient Christmas music blasts above our heads. And I didn't notice it at first, that white noise instrument of my life, the saxophone, leading the cheery music. I imagine someone in the airport, popping a CD into a 5-disc changer (if the airport can't upgrade the bathrooms, why should they upgrade the sound system?), a CD with a title like *Saxy Christmas for Lovers,* or *Smooth R&B Saxophone Holiday Hits, Vol. 23.* It's the saxophone, one song after another, a cruel and punishing loop. Sax, sax, sax. Sleigh bells. Sax. Santa is coming to town. Sax.

Of fucking course.

I begin to think the shuttle bus is not coming. I call the transportation customer service line—something I have literally never done in my life—and ask, nicely, teeth chattering, will it be coming to pick up a group of passengers soon? We'd love to be on our way.

The other passengers eventually ignore me to talk amongst themselves and bob their heads to a jazzy saxophone rendition of "The Little Drummer Boy," and I think, as my heart sinks to the ground covered in fossilized gum, about the way that this is the beginning of the saxophone haunting me for the rest of my life. I'd known, since childhood, that this would be the case someday, and here it was, presenting itself to me like a brick to the face.

What feels like a cruel fact in this moment is that my father had recently released a Christmas album, of better songs than were playing at the airport, of saxophone "hillbilly bebop" covers. If he were there in that moment, standing next to me, he'd hold up his hand, palm out, and make everybody just *sh sh sh! Listen!* so he could diagnose the song, the player, the make and model of the saxophone being played, what kind of reed (synthetic? Cane? Something innovative and new?), what kind of mouthpiece. What kind of recording technique. He could probably venture a guess at the weather conditions on the day of recording. This kind of thing drove me crazy as a kid, being hushed mid-sentence wherever we were—at the mall, or while driving around Birmingham, or while talking during commercial breaks—when a saxophone came on the air; *everybody hush, tch-tch-tch, listen!*

And what I wouldn't give to have him do that very thing, at the airport bus stop where the weather conditions and company are less than ideal. But I do listen. I tilt my head up to the tinny speakers. I don't know what kind of saxophone is being played. I don't know what key. I don't know who the player is, or which horn they are playing. I just know this is the precise moment in which my feelings toward the saxophone become very complex, so I'd better start listening harder. This is when the saxophone begins to follow me everywhere I go. An omen. A blessing. A tableau of grief. Is this what it does to people?

In a way, it's like the saxophone is cursed.

PART I

BEFORE IT WAS COOL

1 DARK ORIGINS

And when at last it was invented in 1842, by Adolphe Sax, a Belgian, it was severely criticized and vilified by many an important critic or a famous conductor. A stillborn invention, doomed to oblivion.

—LEON KOCHNITZKY, *ADOLPHE AND HIS SAXOPHONE* (1949)

The universe tried—hard—to stimy the invention of the saxophone by attempting to bring about the death of a child in nineteenth-century Belgium. Specifically, it targeted Antoine-Joseph (Adolphe) Sax, the eldest of eleven children of Maria Joseph Masson and Charles-Joseph Sax, a celebrated instrument maker. Papa Sax began his career as a cabinet maker and pivoted when he discovered his talents were not in the thrilling world of bespoke cabinetry, but better served in the musical world. His first instrument was a take on the "serpent," an early wind instrument in the brass family that looked precisely like, well, its namesake.

Born in 1814 in Dinant, Belgium, little Adolphe Sax was accident prone to the point of dark comedy; his first great talent was not musical, but poetic in his ability to dodge accidental death. Repeatedly.

In just a few short years, Adolphe had evaded death like it was a superpower. First, he survived a tumble down three flights of stairs, where he smashed his head on a rock floor. He drank sulfuric acid believing it to be milk. He swallowed toxins on three other occasions, with white lead, copper oxide, arsenic, and once—a pin. His head was struck once again by a roof tile, leaving a permanent scar. He fell into a river and nearly drowned. He was badly burned by a gunpowder explosion, and then again by a frying pan. He nearly asphyxiated himself from sleeping near freshly varnished furniture. And these are only a few ways in which the mortal realm wanted Adolphe to quickly ascend to his nickname, given to him by his own mother: "the ghost child."

Little is known about the other Sax children, or Adolphe's mother, Maria Joseph Masson. Her historical record is scant, save for her eleven children (and only four of whom survived into adulthood), and the quote regarding her eldest son, "The child is doomed to suffer; he won't live!"[1]

When your own mother writes you off as doomed, where do you go from there?

---

[1]Wally Horwood, *Adolphe Sax, 1814–1894—His Life and Legacy* (John Heenan, 2014), 420.

Despite young Sax's spectacular talent for near self-destruction, the universe felt he was worth keeping around. His near-fatal childhood hijinks set the stage for Sax's capacity as an eccentric rule-breaker, a nonconformist, and an instigator of conflict enhanced by his hard-won sense of immortality. He taunted the status quo because he always got away with it. In *Adolphe Sax 1814–1891,* Wally Horwood postulates that Sax learned from a young age "he was clearly unable to perceive potential danger in a situation; as a man he was equally oblivious as to the probable reaction of others to his initiatives."[2]

Adolphe was born into musical talent, but unlike his father, he didn't try his hand at cabinets first. Music ran through his veins, a savior pushing him through a tumultuous life. He learned his father's trade, gaining advanced shop skills during his teen years. He formally studied the clarinet and flute at the Royal School of Singing and began dabbling in instrument-making by working on an update to the bass clarinet. He turned the crass instrument into a sophisticated woodwind by changing its bore and location of the instrument's holes. Young Sax spent years further experimenting with the clarinet, concocting a prototype of a single-reed instrument that boasted the powerful sound of a brass instrument with all the dexterity of a woodwind.

Sax's bass clarinet featured a large bore (interior chamber), a straight tube to replace the curves of the serpent, cups to

[2]Ibid, 439.

cover the holes, twenty-two keys, and a bell that faced the floor, alternately curving upward to carry the sound forward. Sax was also a gifted musician, playing his new instrument in reputable musical societies, including *La Grande Harmonie Royale* and the Philharmonic Society. Other players became jealous of Sax—the beginning of a trend that followed him until death. A clarinetist of *Grande Harmonie Royale,* M. Bachman, went so far as to say if the society adopted Sax's instrument (meaning he'd have to play it), he'd quit. So, as one does, Sax challenged him to a musical dual. Sax won and was appointed as the bass clarinetist to the *Grande Harmonie Royale* and the Philharmonic Society.

After getting a taste of success, Sax decided that Brussels wasn't the place to be for a talented and industrious inventor such as he (particularly when he was denied the top prize in the Brussels Exhibition of 1841, despite the judges' admitted superiority of his works), so he packed up his instruments and moved to Paris in 1842 at age twenty-eight. He was poor in a monetary sense but rich in ambition.

Sax's reputation and confidence preceded him. He used his charms and talent to make friends in high places in the music world, befriending top-tier composers such as Berlioz, Halevy, and Meyerbeer. And it was Berlioz who wrote of Sax's bass clarinet, making the public aware while creating demand for his near-perfect musical specimens.

Just as Charles Sax had devoted his life to rearing and supporting his large family, so, too, did Adolphe Sax in expanding a family of instruments to encompass more registers and support orchestras. In 1843 he filed patents for six horns—known as saxhorns—and six valve horns in 1845 that he called saxtrombas. These were followed by patents for eight variations of saxophones in 1846, and a family of saxtubas in 1849. In his prolific career, Adolphe Sax patented a whopping forty-six instruments.[3] Clearly, he had a thing for patents.

In all his ingenuity, Sax also seemed to have a thing in the art of making enemies. The first known opposer to what is believed to be the prototype of the saxophone was an unknown person who, moments before the Brussels Industrial Exhibition of 1841, kicked the horn across the floor with such force that it had to be withdrawn from display. Three years later, the instrument emerged into the public eye. Berlioz penned a flowery description introducing the invention, describing it as, "a brass instrument with nineteen keys, whose shape is rather similar to the ophicleide. . . . The Saxophone becomes the head of a new group; that of the brass instruments with reed. . . . Its sound is of such rare quality that, to my knowledge, there is not a bass instrument in use nowadays that could be compared to the Saxophone. It is full soft, vibrating, extremely powerful, and easy to lower in intensity."[4]

---

[3]"The Invention of the Saxophone by the Great Adolphe Sax." Henri Selmer Paris. Accessed June 16, 2024. https://www.selmer.fr/en/blogs/infos/invention-du-saxophone-par-adolphe-sax#:~:text=His%20goal%20was%20to%20cover,instruments%20known%20as%20the%20saxtrombas.
[4]Wally Horwood, *Adolphe Sax 1814–1894* (John Heenan, 2014), Loc 852.

It was also Berlioz who wrote of Sax's family of instruments to a wide audience, in *Journal des Debats,* in 1842. As a conductor and prose writer, Berlioz was the nineteenth century equivalent of a social media influencer. His promotional writing about his friend's talents did not go unnoticed. Sax became an overnight success in the music world of Paris, performing for captivated audiences. The problem was that adoration alone did not pay the bills. Sax was broke. He went without food for days and lived in the cheapest apartments he could find. When he was offered a loan to build a workshop, Sax graciously accepted. He scraped by during these years, spending what money he had on his workshop—often described as a glorified shed—and the expensive materials needed to make brass and woodwind instruments.

His business did well, to the disdain of the other instrument makers in the area. Sax made friends in high places, but he made enemies in equal measure. Local instrument makers did not appreciate an outsider butting his way into the inner circle, and Sax had charged in like a bull with no apologies. After only a few months of operations in his ramshackle factory, Sax's valved trumpets gained the attention of the French army, who had a less than stellar reputation compared to their Prussian and Austrian counterparts. He also piqued the interest of Gaetano Donizetti, a composer who wrote the opera, *Don Sebastian,* with the Sax bass clarinet in mind in 1843. This did not go over well with his orchestra, because many of the players were close with competing manufacturers and refused to play a Sax instrument. According to these players, Sax's instruments were faulty specimens. Sax was no stranger to a musical duel, so he once again challenged one of the players to an instrument showdown, but the player turned him down. Instead Sax offered to sit in and play the piece himself; the musicians threatened a mass exodus. Donizetti had to bend to the will of his orchestra.

On the plus side, the *Don Sebastian* incident gave Sax free publicity.

Behind the scenes, Sax was having trouble retaining employees. He'd painstakingly train them how to make his superior instruments, then they'd be lured away to competitors, taking those proprietary secrets with them. His workshop was broken into on several occasions, tools were stolen, and works in progress destroyed. He was denied credit to get the expensive raw materials needed to make instruments. He'd be harassed for breach of contract if he missed any delivery dates. It's as though he couldn't sneeze without being slapped with bad fortune.

It only makes sense that Sax's history of skirting death would come back around to knock on his door, like he was living his own endless loop of *Final Destination*. As an adult, death came for him in the form of an incendiary device meant to toast him while he slept. Alas, the fuse was too short, and the explosion was premature. Another: a physical attack in which Sax escaped through bravery and charm. Another: in 1845, one of Sax's trusted and devoted employees was murdered, having been mistaken for Sax by the unknown attacker and stabbed through the heart. This loss devastated Sax.

The more I learn about Adolphe Sax, the more I question the topography of his mind. I wonder if he was missing some small synapse that signals self-preservation—or if he had something extra knocking around in there that propelled his ambitions beyond mere mortals.

He threw himself wholeheartedly into his obsessions. He didn't consider the consequences of what he believed to be the greater good of the musical world. Nothing was more important than sound. Money, of course, was a frequent concern. Sax was easily swindled out of 4,000 francs and a lien on his factory by a thief promising him a loan. The blows to his business became too much for Sax; instead of facing the dishonorable mark of bankruptcy, he contemplated suicide. It's easy to imagine what turmoil Sax must have been going through, with his ambition and passions slashed by rivals, his success met with aggression and loathing at every turn.

Fortunately, Sax had friends and enthusiastic fans. A French army general and longtime supporter of Sax's instruments, De Rumigny, convinced Queen Marie-Amelie, wife of Louis-Phillipe, to pay off Sax's creditors. His workshop was back in business. He met regularly with fellow musicians, discussed music theory, and played concerts with them, which is how he gained the attention of writers, government officials, and scientists. Despite his lack of monetary success, Sax was making his fortune in other ways.

The first public showing of the saxophone (tenor) was at the Paris Industrial Exhibition of 1844. Despite winning over the jury, Sax took home the silver medal. Perhaps he didn't secure the gold because he was too good a player—the judges considered that his talent as a musician eclipsed his talent as an inventor, thereby making the saxophone sound better than it was. Of course, Sax found that ridiculous, saying, "If you praise me as a player rather than an inventor, and as here only invention is important, then I shall withdraw. I came only because I could find nobody able or willing to play the instrument."[5]

For every roadblock thrown in front of Sax, there also came praise. People considered the saxophone godlike, ethereal, not of this world. Composer Michele Carafa was enamored with the instrument, saying it was the most beautiful sound he had ever heard. In fact, he composed a military band piece, *La Corona d'Italia,* for King Victor Emmanuel II in 1868 with the saxophone in mind. He loved Sax's work so much, that a band composed entirely of his instruments played Beethoven's Funeral March at Carafa's funeral.

Throughout Sax's lifetime, themes emerge. He finds success and praise with his inventions and improvements on existing instruments, then is met with great jealousy and opposition. Devoted friends lift him out of the tight positions

---

[5]Wally Horwood, *Adolphe Sax 1814–1894—His Life and Legacy* (John Heenan, 2014), 1118.

he inevitably finds himself in, and something befalls him again—all the while, death lurks around the corner, watching him with narrowed eyes.

In 1845, Sax built a 45-instrument army band, in direct competition with Michele Carafa, the composer of whom would later become a total fan boy of his rival. Twenty-thousand spectators showed up to watch the spectacle of whose army band would make the cut. Sax was included in the band, having no choice but to strap two instruments to his chest, as a handful of his players had been coerced away before they were to take the stage. They played brilliantly, despite being seven players short and largely rejected by the audience, who did not seem to take a liking to the "foreigner" that had dared to represent a better military band with his sonorous and beautiful instruments. Some threw rocks. Despite the haters (some things never change), there was no denying that Sax's band was superior. His instruments—including saxhorns and saxophones—found a place in the revamped infantry and cavalry bands. At the age of thirty, Sax had found himself at the top of the Parisian music world. He'd achieved the approval of the highest order, which allowed him to expand his shabby workshop to accommodate the influx of instruments he'd be making. Investors clamored to get a piece of the pie. His workshop concerts and friendly discussions brought standing-room-only crowds.

While Sax celebrated his acclaim, his rivals formed an association which served the purpose of reclaiming their livelihoods, which they felt Sax had singlehandedly stolen from them. It wasn't hard to figure out Sax's greatest weakness. He was an artist and a performer, not a businessman. They set out to drive him to bankruptcy and ruin his name. They also sought to strip him of his patents. Worse, they criticized the saxophone, claiming its sound to be offensive, monstrous, and blaring. And to make matters worse, the political climate would take a turn, sending Paris into near-anarchy as it deposed Louis-Phillipe as king during the revolution. The military bands were directed to reform back to their old, clunky ways. Sax's workshop was piled high with unwanted instruments. Another brush with death saw Sax and his friends lined up in the street and ordered to be shot for supposedly firing weapons at soldiers. A general arrived and interfered with the execution because he recognized Sax and knew he was no enemy to the regime.

In 1852, the benefactor that had kept Sax's workshop afloat all those years ago died. The man's daughter and heiress to his fortune went against her father's wishes and went after Sax for the 30,000 francs she felt was owed back to her family. Sax, ever the honest man no matter how many troubles it brought to his door, did not deny the loan. He signed a paper stating the fact and was given a day to repay it. In 1852 terms, 30,000 francs equaled about $33,400 USD. In 2024 terms, that was roughly 1.4 million bucks. Sax was screwed. He filed for bankruptcy.

Sax was no stranger to the courts. The association of his rivals kept him in litigation for years; no sooner would Sax win a case (often by the ironclad strength of his patents), would they drag him back for another round. Imagine what feats these men might have accomplished had they hobbies of their own. They claimed the Sax family of instruments were not new or special in any way—with the added insult of Sax stamping his name on them—and wanted his patents to be cancelled immediately, that he be fined 100 francs for making it all up and deceiving everyone. It must have also been a great frustration for the people of the courts to bear witness to such feuding as these men, such tenacity, over *musical instruments.*

In Sax's defense, his supporters gave speeches about his honorable character. Worse, they summoned pity by claiming Sax was in such hock that he'd considered pawning medals he won at Exhibitions. To judge him negatively was, in essence, the same as judging the future of art, and by stifling progress, it would be to the detriment of all society. The complainants argued it wasn't fair for one man to hold a monopoly on groups of instruments they felt he did not invent, and that his success relied heavily on the influence of his famous friends; in fact, the saxophone never happened, what nonsense, what fodder! Above all, he should not be allowed to hold a patent on the saxophone because he played it in public before filing the paperwork, so that meant it was public property. The flaw here is that the opposition argued both as inscrutable truths: First, that the saxophone never existed. Second, that the saxophone was played in front of the public—therefore it belongs to everyone! It's Schrödinger's cat, it both does and does not exist until we open the instrument case.

The case was dismissed and appealed by the jilted association. Another case argued that Sax clearly had no faith in his patented inventions because he had ordered patents for the minimum number of years instead of the maximum. The truth is Sax was too poor to pay the hefty fees associated with longer terms. That he was an immoral "bachelor" did not uphold their family-focused ideals. The petty arguments and accusations went on for eight years. Despite winning his cases, Sax's name had been dragged through the mud.

Little is known about Sax's personal life. Despite his status as a bachelor married to his work, he did have a partner and children. He lost a child and a sibling within days of each other. His aging parents moved in with him. At 39, Sax discovered a dark spot on his lip. He was given a prescription of rest. When that inevitably failed, other remedies were tried with no success. A year passed and his lip had grown so swollen he couldn't chew his food. Within five years, the spot had grown to such a size that doctors finally diagnosed the advanced melanoma, which spread to his jaw. Sax was promised a painful and difficult death, with a small chance of survival if they removed his lip and part of his jaw. The surgery was delayed so that Sax could attend Court for another one of his myriad lawsuits.

Sax faced two choices. He could live with a disfigurement that would not only affect his appearance but kill his musical ability. Or he could die a painful death as the cancer suffocated him from the inside. He consulted a friend who told him about an Indian doctor in Paris, named Dr. Vries, that had miraculously cured hopeless cases. Vries placed Sax on a strict diet and prescribed a mysterious cocktail of herbs. It didn't work. Sax's throat began to close, and he had to be fed through a tube. He was so miserable that he attempted suicide. Dr. Vries insisted that he stay the course. In 1859, six years into his cancer diagnosis, the cancer shrank, eventually leaving his body and lip entirely without a trace, as though the curse had been lifted.

Aside from his lowest days, Sax never stopped tinkering and dreaming of new instruments. He drew up plans for new instruments and was always looking for ways to improve valve systems. He went down a rabbit hole of producing bass instruments so large as to become impractical pieces of art rather than something a human could carry around, let alone produce sound while trying to tame the six-and-a-half-foot beast. Cartoonists went wild with this one, liking it to being mistaken for the building one might enter to see the instrument on exhibit. Sax was quick to retort, "Next year, I shall exhibit an instrument with the diameter of the *Colonne de Juillet* and I shall call it 'Saxothunder.'"[6]

Picture it—SAXOTHUNDER!—all the airbrush t-shirt opportunities.

The highest honor awarded to Sax was the *Grand Prix*, in 1857 at the Paris Exhibition. He displayed one piece of every instrument he'd invented or improved, including an alto saxophone plated in gold. It is after this point that we reluctantly follow Sax into the downward trajectory of the rest of his life.

---

[6]Wally Horwood, *Adolphe Sax 1814–1894—His Life and Legacy* (John Heenan, 2014), 2925.

In 1862, Sax came down with a lung infection. It was recommended he move away from the fumes of Paris and into the woods, where the air was cleaner. It was out of the question for him to leave his factory. Instead, he invented an air purifier full of antiseptic, which did the trick. After proudly serving as a member of the Legion of Honour under Emperor Napoleon III, Sax was stripped of the title because the committee had somehow missed his imperfect financial situation—a person could not receive this rank with a bankruptcy on record. After his patents lapsed, Sax's inventions were now open to any manufacturer to commodify, so his business dwindled. He lost three of his most influential friends, including Berlioz, within the span of four years. Despite his awards and court cases ruled in his favor, Sax was not paid for either of these things, leading to his second bankruptcy. He came to agreements with his creditors and stayed afloat another few years, until filing bankruptcy for a third time in 1877, at age 63. There was no way around it. Sax was forced to sell his instrument collection, a catalog of 467 pieces. These included his beloved saxophones, and the pieces that had given him success. It must have been a low emotional point for him—everything he'd worked so hard to achieve, and to keep out of the hands of those that wanted to stifle the evolution of music itself— had to be sold to the highest bidder. The collection earned him a mere 12,000 francs. He attempted to bounce back and enter another exhibition in 1878, but was unable to afford the entry fee, so he watched as other entrants demonstrated variations of the instruments he invented. The saxophones were among the winners.[7]

Sax had to give up his workshop-factory in rue Saint-Georges for a smaller outfit and continued to move around over the years as he tried to keep up with the payments on his debts while trying to keep his business open. His son, Adolphe-Edouard, is believed to have taken over the family business toward the end of Sax's life. In the end, Sax lived off a small pension of 300 francs from a musician's organization of which he'd been an active member throughout his career—and even this, had to come at the petition of his fellow musicians who felt a great debt was owed to Sax for what he gave the world. But still, at such a socioeconomically low level, Sax undoubtedly lived out his last years with the help of his son. He tried to make a public appeal for damages caused to his business, finances, and character over the years, at the hands of his venomous rivals. He wanted resolution so that "this would permit me before dying to pay others what I owe them, and give myself a few hours of peace in a life consumed by trouble."[8]

The musical society of Paris took pity on Sax, recognizing the irony that Sax made incredible things in his lifetime,

---

[7]Stephen Cottrell, *The Saxophone* (New Haven: Yale University Press, 2013), 34–35.

[8]K.N. Deans. "A Comprehensive Performance Project in Saxophone Literature with an Essay Consisting of Translated Source Readings in the Life and Work of Adolphe Sax." Doctoral dissertation, University of Iowa, 1980.

for which other men became millionaires. He died in his home on February 7, 1894, at the age of, in Paris. He was buried in the family tomb in Montmartre cemetery. His obituary across the globe, in the *New-York Tribune,* reads in bold: "Antoine Joseph Sax died from pneumonia here to-day, in absolute poverty."[9] Other obituaries read much of the same, listing Sax's incredible accomplishments while overshadowing them with the fact of his destitution. The closing of his obituary in the London *Times* reads as particularly jabbing: "He reformed modern orchestras, and yet died poor."[10]

Adolphe-Edouard continued his father's legacy as long as he could muster, taking over his father's post as the director of the stage music at the Paris Opera and continued as an instrument manufacturer. He built a new factory in Paris and kept the company afloat until 1929, when it was sold to Selmer, today's most premiere saxophone manufacturer.

Adolphe Sax lived quite the life and left us with a legacy that shouldn't be forgotten, so long as the saxophone continues to carry his name. From his humble beginnings as the ghost child, dodging death at every turn, Sax became a legend who added dodging murder, lawsuits, haters of the saxophone, and ruinous men, to his docket. He is largely written about in a romantic way, which is fitting because that moment in time witnessed the height of the Romantic period. He became the

---

[9] *New-York Tribune,* February 10, 1894, 12.
[10] *The Times,* February 10, 1894, 5.

butt of the jokes of satirists, appearing in satirical cartoons damning he never be forgiven. In a roundabout way, Sax's enemies exhausted themselves attempting to ruin his name, when all they had to do was let him do it himself.

It's easy to stare at the handful of photographs and depictions of Adolphe Sax. The modern camera would not come for another hundred years or so. Electricity wasn't really a common thing, either. The two photographs most easily surfaced of Adolphe Sax were taken about a decade apart. The first displays a confident man with bedroom eyes, maybe early thirties, wearing a frock coat and crisp white shirt, bowtie, a thick beard with a mustache brushing against his heart-shaped upper lip. He has a sharp, long nose, heavy black eyebrows, and carefully quaffed hair that curls over his ears. There's a faintly haunted facial expression that follows him through the years to the next portrait; wearing a suit that looks a bit more threadbare and worn than his younger portrayal. His face is rounded with age, hairline an inch or two above his eyes, squinting as if looking for the bright side of things.

It's like he's still looking, all these centuries later.

2 THE SOUND

The saxophone was the result of Adolphe Sax's desire to phonetically solve the problem of the ophicleide and the bassoon. Ophicleides, all but extinct today, produce a sound far too mighty for an enclosed room, with the bassoon having the opposite problem of low whispers. Sax wanted to find balance between them, a pleasant output that could be heard *and* endured. His solution was to fit a single-reed mouthpiece to the body of the ophicleide—conjectured by historians to be a mouthpiece taken from a bass clarinet, and thus the saxophone was born.[1]

There are book-length masterpieces about the machinations of the saxophone and its siblings. They're detailed on a scientific, granular, microscopic level. I'm neither granular, scientific, nor a subject-matter expert on how this instrument works. I only know from reading and notating those tome-like books, talking to people, and condensing it all for the sake of brevity and whimsy. There's

---

[1]Stephen Cottrell, *The Saxophone* (New Haven: Yale University Press, 2013), 41.

your warning—I'm only able to scratch the surface of the brass here.

There are four mainstream classes of the modern saxophone: alto, soprano, tenor, and baritone. Lesser known but not uncommon models include sopranino and bass, contrabass and sub-contra bass. Most variations of this instrument are made up of a body, a neck, and a cork sleeve in which to attach the mouthpiece. Each achieves its own sound, higher or lower, depending on the instrument's size, though all are notated the same.

Of the four popular variations of the saxophone, the soprano has the highest and brightest pitch (B♭)—and is often mistaken for a clarinet in looks, with its straight body and neck. The alto, which I always referred to as "the baby tenor" when I was too young to know better, is smaller in size than a tenor but looks similar, its pitch the mildest in range (E♭). The alto is the most agreeable of saxophones, often finding itself a common place in beginner bands. Its bigger sibling, the tenor, is a beloved and iconic instrument in jazz. The lower pitch (B♭) and versatility of the tenor gives its player the freedom to explore a range of dark and bright sounds. And the baritone on the lowest range (E♭) lends a large presence—over three feet tall when assembled, a loop in the bell, and has the deepest, bassiest voice of all saxophones. Because of its weight and stature, the baritone can be a tough one to master.

With its conical bore, the saxophone overblows at the octave, not unlike an oboe. Twelve keys rest open, while the other tone holes are covered when not used. If you look at a diagram of a saxophone, it's easy to imagine how Adolphe Sax spent years perfecting the tone hole placements while also keeping it functional to the human hands. It's wild to consider Sax did all of this, toiling away in his factory without the luxury of modern electricity, creating these instruments from scratch.

A lot of work goes into making a saxophone. Today's Selmer alto takes thirty hours of work to produce, with 850 parts to be assembled by sixteen different professionals in their specialties. It starts with sheets of brass, copper, and zinc, cut to a pattern to fit the bell, body, neck, and bow. The pieces are hammered, pressed, and welded together. Then the body is shaped into a conical bore, into which the tone holes are cut. The neck is carefully shaped after being dipped in a water and alcohol bath and bent into shape. From there, the keys and various pieces are attached, and everything is polished and lacquered. The intricate engravings on the horns are done by hand. Each instrument is tuned before sending it off to its new owner.[2]

In an article evangelizing the saxophone in *Journal des debates* in 1842, Berlioz described the sounds of the instrument as relating to the cello, clarinet, and the English horn, with "the timbre of the high notes of the low saxophone

---

[2] Henri SELMER Paris, "History & making of the saxophone," YouTube, April 26, 2021, accessed June 26, 2024, https://youtu.be/z-GDrCxcV80?si=QfxXy-0HMtKXV6OP.

has something of pain and sorrow, whereas that of their bass notes has, so to speak, an imposing, papal calm."[3] Over a hundred years later, we're still finding much of the same, that, "It cries, sighs and dreams. It possesses a crescendo and can gradually diminish its sound until it is only an echo of an echo of an echo—until its sound becomes crepuscular."[4]

Mouthpieces are a whole other beast. They are procured separately from the instrument, and there is no shortage in variety; each provides a different tone, feel, and quality. It's up to the player to decide what personality they're going for. At the underside of every mouthpiece is a baffle, the shape of which plays a huge role in tonal quality. The reed—what gives the saxophone its technical designation as a woodwind instrument—is attached to the mouthpiece with a ligature. The most common type of reed is cane, though synthetic reeds are also common. And there are many options for mouthpieces for which a player can tinker until they find the range that suits their embouchure—or position of the lips over the mouthpiece. The mouthpiece can make even a lower-end horn sound a bit more special.

I want to know more about the world of mouthpieces, so I reach out to Mark Sepinuck, owner and manufacturer of 10MFAN Mouthpieces. Sepinuck has dedicated his life

---

[3]Berlioz, "Instrument[s] de Musique: M. Adolphe Sax." *Journal des debates*, June 12, 1842, revised 1860, 284.

[4]Michael Segell, *The Devil's Horn: The Story of the Saxophone, from Noisy Novelty to King of Cool* (New York: Farrar, Straus and Giroux, 2005), 14.

to the saxophone, starting as a player and educator before becoming a mouthpiece manufacturer. For three decades, he was the largest online dealer of vintage mouthpieces. In 2013, he began creating his own, each offering a unique tone distinct from any vintage mouthpiece before it. Where other manufactures might make a small tweak to a classic vintage piece, he wanted to do something different. He tells me, "they blow like a 10MFAN mouthpiece and not a vintage Otto Link, Selmer, or Meyer, for example. They have their own special sauce. That's why people like—or don't like—them."

Players around the globe love 10MFAN mouthpieces because of those special sounds. It's all about finding the perfect fit, and as he explains the idea to me, I am reminded of the wand selection experience in *Harry Potter*—Sepinuck knows just the mouthpiece to suit the player. He's what I call the mouthpiece whisperer; he'll keep at it until he finds just the right fit. "Sometimes, I get emails from guys that have been playing for 40 years and are looking for something different, a sound color[5] that gives them something more," he says. "Then I give them recommendations, send them a mouthpiece. They'll come back and say, 'Hey, that's the sound I've been looking for for 40 years!'"

10MFAN mouthpieces are categorized numerically from one to three, tailored to each horn type, size, and tone. If the

---

[5]Sound color, also known as tone color or timbre, is the unique sound that distinguishes one instrument from another. A fun lesson: https://study.com /learn/lesson/what-is-tone-color-definition-examples.html.

musician is seeking a mouthpiece similar to a vintage piece, Sepinuck knows where to start, because those vintage designs are what inspire him to create new ones. His mouthpieces are nuanced in warmth, edge, brightness, and power. Sepinuck explains it to me as, a saxophonist might be playing in a quiet venue with a guitar player, and they're going for the warmth of Stan Getz; they'd start with category one. Category two has more punch, like a Dexter Gordon sound. Category three has all the brightness, edginess, and the power of Clarence Clemons on stage with Bruce Springsteen. But he's dedicated to more than just finding a sax player the right mouthpiece to get them a "sound"—he wants them to have a great experience along the way.

My dad played category three 10MFAN mouthpieces— power, brightness, edge—and was more than a fan of the brand, he was a friend. Sepinuck has that effect on people; he's kind, humble, and passionate about the saxophone. And he makes a damn good mouthpiece. He doesn't offer new mouthpieces until he's prototyped and thoroughly tested them; sometimes that process can take months. My dad talked about the new mouthpieces to me all the time and his enthusiasm was palpable. Now I see why. I may not play the sax, but Sepinuck explains it to me as going beyond sound. It's bigger than that, in the same way that it is true within any creative community; it's more about being in the business of being a good art, literary, or music citizen.

Sepinuck's passion and joy for what he does is genuine, which has made his brand beloved among saxophonists. "I don't care if you're brand new to the saxophone or you're Coltrane—you're after the same thing," he tells me. "I'll talk to a stranger on the phone for an hour and ask them, what is it you want to do that you can't do now? I'll help you get there. I don't treat anyone different, which is how it should be. That's my job, and that's what I'm here to do."

Sepinuck reminds me that it isn't about the instruments, the type of horns, or the mouthpieces to get you to a sound. It's about the music that we are left with—and that lasts forever.

SHEET MUSIC #1: RAISED BY A SAX MAN

There is a line spoken by a character in *Twin Peaks,* "The Man From Another Place": "Where we're from the birds sing a pretty song . . . and there's always music in the air." He is talking about the Black Lodge—neither heaven nor hell, but a kind of liminal purgatory, where people linger for indeterminate amounts of time. Purgatory is what I consider the house to be in Pell City where I grew up, a rural Alabama town where about 8,000 people lived during the 1990s. Now, it's considered a large suburb of Birmingham (a big deal: they have a T.J. Maxx *and* a Cracker Barrel now). The house was 800 square feet, red brick, two bedroom, one bathroom, with a soggy back yard framed by a fence I helped my dad build when I was eleven or twelve.

The living room and bedroom floors of this house slowly caved in over the years, creating a bouncy-house effect, but did nothing to diminish the sound quality of the seven-foot Magneplanar flat-panel music speakers that were a staple in our daily lives. When my dad wasn't practicing his saxophone in a bedroom, door closed though it hardly made a difference, he was playing CDs through a complicated stack of machinery attached to the speakers as they grazed our living room ceiling. Music *was* always in the air. I didn't realize until years later that most small children aren't sent running to the closet to get away from the terrifying, huge sounds of Pink Floyd's *Dark Side of the Moon*.

Being the kid of a devoted saxophonist means learning how to listen to music with a trained ear, and perhaps most importantly, how to have a sense of humor. Greg, my dad, was also raised in Pell City, the son of a newspaper editor and mean drunk. The house Greg grew up in was filled with music—sax players like Ace Cannon and Boots Randolph. He started playing the saxophone in the sixth grade, after ignoring the advice from his third-grade teacher that told him he "wasn't musical" and "shouldn't mess with it." He went on to win First Chair in national competitions in junior high and high school, and when he was sixteen, in 1973, he was invited to play in the United States Collegiate Wind Band in Europe and Russia. I wish I knew more about this trip. The only story I know, for certain, is that at some point during this trip he leaned against a hotel sink, and broke it, in Amsterdam. Whether he participated in other activities, I can only speculate.

He went through the motions of college at Jacksonville State University, getting a degree in playing classical music, though all he cared about was being part of the band, the Marching Southerners. The Southerners are one of the most prestigious collegiate marching bands. He told me later that he was nervous about leaving college because it meant having to do something other than play saxophone. His life had been on autopilot until this point. He began his career as a young band director in nearby Ragland. He met a girl in church, and his path was set.

Our house in Pell City may have been falling apart inside, with its sinking floors, Pepto-pink bedroom walls, and bowing shower walls, but the outside was solid red brick. Solid enough to stand against countless tornado warnings, the sirens wailing like banshees. The electricity went out whenever the wind blew too hard. But to live in the South is to be no stranger to thunderstorms and lightning zapping your electronics. The stereo system was the first thing my dad unplugged when that first drop of rain thumped against the tin roof.

Greg was a school band director whose income was enough to afford us—a family of four, a small house on a country road, and an old Chevy Lumina. By today's standards and housing market, that's incredible. We had it all, even though sometimes we paid for gas and candy bars with quarters and dimes. Yet somehow, there was always enough money to keep the house in music. I ran around the house singing along to "The Girl From Ipanema" as my dad sat in the center of his sound setup, leaning one ear to the side, studying Getz's cool-yet-detached saxophone work, as though he hadn't already listened to it thousands of times. This was a quirk I inherited from my dad: studying something repeatedly, trying to understand and pick apart how someone did something I loved. For him, it was recording techniques, saxophone solos, pitch, and registers.

For me, it's books, essays, writers—art is a puzzle I am always trying to solve for myself. I learned all about obsession in that little brick house of music, mostly from my dad's saxophones. The saxophones were as much a part of him as his wedding ring, his favorite pair of New Balance shoes, or his ancient shaving cream cup shaped like a pig. He never got angry when I interrupted his daily practicing, and he'd encourage me to press the saxophone keys ("Can I push the buttons?" I'd ask, eager to own the sound), making all manner of racket that was probably the reason some of our neighbors avoided us—or the records and CDs blasting through, clear and bright through an elegant sound system in a non-elegant locale.

We'd spent hours combing through CDs at Sam Goody or Magic Platter in Birmingham, leaving the stores with a small bag each. I was spoiled in music. I had two snaking CD towers in my room that were balanced by notebooks to keep them from tipping over on the crooked hardwood floor. I got my first 3-disc changer stereo in 1998; I blasted Nine Inch Nails and Third Eye Blind in my room while my dad blasted Cannonball Adderley or Michael Brecker in the next. My sister focused on makeup and sketching, and my mother focused on Jesus, doll collecting, and QVC. We didn't hunt, fish, or go to the Nascar races one town over in Talladega. We went to Books-A-Million and every music shop in Birmingham. Pell City didn't really know what to do with us.

In 2016, when I was head-first in love with my side hustle as a journalist in Sacramento, I decided to practice my inquisitiveness on my father. He'd been a musician my whole life, and I'd never considered it as unusual, odd, or anything worth investigating. But the more I interviewed artists, actors, and comedians, the more I realized my dad was interesting as hell. Such few people have obsessions that become their personality. I had taken it for granted. But my dad lived a complicated life, torn between his obsession and paying his bills. Being a sax man, much like being a writer, was not lucrative. He pawned his horns a handful of times. He usually got them back. He had a Selmer—the gold standard of saxophones—but I don't know what happened to it. He acquired, and sold, many mouthpieces and equipment on eBay. Not playing the saxophone was never a logical option or even a minor consideration. It was breathing.

I called him one day and used my journalist tactics to prod him about the history of his sax playing. I wanted him to realize how interesting and talented he really was. He'd spent his life in the shadow of the church, being talked down to by people closest to him in the name of the Lord, and sometimes I wondered if he felt something like failure. He told me only a few things about his childhood, his life spent going to church with his buddies and being bored out of his mind. Eventually he found a loophole to the boredom: he could play saxophone on a stage. "Once I started playing, that was it. Once it's an obsession, that's all you do."

3 EVERYONE IS LAUGHING

In 1923, a young E.B. White, freshly relieved of his journalist duties from the *Seattle Times*, hopped aboard a steamer ship bound for Alaska. He paid his way on this voyage by taking odd jobs on the ship as they came available. He was young, free, and not burdened with anything as ridiculous as money trouble, though he probably should have been. In his essay, "The Years of Wonder," White is dazzled by the onboard entertainment, the Six Brown Brothers, a vaudeville sextet of brothers that each played a saxophone. Their style was vaudevillian, setting the stage for the saxophone to take the front and center as a clown. Really. The brothers performed in clown suits and are to this day credited as having a large role in bringing the saxophone to American audiences. White describes the scene in St. Lawrence as the Brothers unleashed their "sweet jazz" to a local crowd, that the Brothers "unlimbered their horns, and the Eskimos [*sic*] danced, with surprising frenzy. None of them had ever heard a sax, and the sound made them drunk."[1]

---

[1] E.B. White, "The Years of Wonder," *The Essays of E.B. White* (New York: HarperCollins, 2014) 344.

By the time White took his Alaskan voyage, the saxophone had already become the star of traveling circus and variety acts such as the Brown Brothers and The Musical Spillers, having made a name for itself as a novelty or comedy instrument—far removed from the legacy that Adolphe Sax envisioned for his iconic instrument. On the other hand, he may have relished in the splendor and drama as the lovers and haters of the saxophone continued to vehemently argue over its place in modern music.

The odd serpentine shape and unfamiliar sound of the saxophone certainly did not help its reputation in being taken seriously in the early nineteenth century. It *looked* like an object made for comedy, with its swan shape, flapping keys, and long neck. It was loud. It fit the personality of vaudeville like a glove. It was an easy enough instrument to pick up and play, and easier when the musician used it as a prop instead of a vehicle for music, making the sax "laugh" and "cry" along with whatever scenario played out for the people wearing the clown suits. Even Tom Brown, the head of the Brown Brothers, played the leading role while dressed as a clown in blackface, as a nod to the popular portrayals in minstrel shows deeply rooted in racism. No wonder the saxophone has had such a long, strange career; it's often found itself at the center of the most tumultuous and embarrassing times in history.

The saxophone straddled the fence for the first two decades of the twentieth century. It didn't go straight from the hands of Adolphe Sax to John Coltrane. First, it went through the red-light district of New Orleans (Storyville), until it was shut down by the US Navy in 1917. And the 1920s seemed to dispute the question: was it funny, or was it art? While the vaudeville acts were focused on making people laugh and keeping them entertained with the ragtime style, serious musicians were tired of the lack of respect that the saxophone had gained, all its charms being used for low brow and cheap entertainment.

Clay Smith and G.E. Holmes, a pair of instrumentalists that made a name for themselves on circus and vaudeville stages, wanted everyone to consider them—and most importantly, the saxophone—serious and respectable. Smith demanded the word "novelty" not appear in any of their advertising. This, though Smith and Holmes ran their own vaudeville company. They believed, like Adolphe Sax, the instrument belonged in the orchestra pit. In a column they wrote for *The Dominant* in 1917, they boldly claim the saxophone, "If played well it has a fine tone quality, which blends admirably with the modern orchestrations. But God save us from the hideous cat-calling that is so much in vogue at the present termed 'Jassing.' . . . Really, the 'Jasser' should be subject to the same quarantine restrictions as if he had the foot and mouth disease."[2]

While the variety groups were learning to play saxophone with one hand—so as to free the other for

---

[2] Clay Smith and G.E. Holmes, "Saxophone Article," *The Dominant* 24 (January 1917), 80–81.

juggling—Rudy Wiedoeft was enjoying widespread fame as a sax player with remarkable talent for fast fingering, rapid tongue techniques, and smooth playing, often gaining more applause for his position in the pit than the main stage acts. His specialty was with the C-melody saxophone, which was immensely popular in the first quarter of the century—odd, considering Adolphe Sax had intended it for orchestral use—though it fell out of favor and has not been in production since the 1930s, Wiedoeft's control of the C-melody landed him recording sessions as a soloist and contributor to dance records, as a leader of the Master Saxophone Sextet, an orchestral accompanist, and a composer. He was outspoken about his desire to be seen as a serious musician, and he publicly shamed saxophonists who picked up the instrument without learning how to properly play it, instead going for the "weird" novelty sounds over tone, scales, and intonation. Of course, once one knows the rules, they can break them, and Wiedoeft was gifted in that way.

Though outspoken on his disdain for novelty or comedic sax players, Wiedoeft was considered among their best and brightest. It comes as no surprise to any artist or musician that often one must go where the money is, and he was no exception, though it pained him to confess: "with a spirit of unwillingness that I have made 'jazz' records, or played this type of solo, but it was also true that this is what many people want to hear on the saxophone. . . . I have endeavored to produce weird effects, such as glissando, tongue-flutter,

'Oriental,' etc. with the least possible sacrifice of dignity of the instrument."[3]

Little is known about women's role in the early days of the saxophone (typical), but around the time of the women's suffragette movement, all-female groups ranging from four to twenty women formed all-saxophone bands.[4] This would have been met with potentially negative results, as it was uncommon and seen as "improper" for women to play instruments publicly.

The "saxophone craze" years were long, from 1900 to 1930, the sharp decline signaled by the Great Depression, which rocked the country and where few could afford the luxury of live entertainment. The saxophone made its way into big bands, was a staple of the dance clubs, and it was trendy to pick up and learn how to make it parrot laughter, crying, bullfrog moans, champagne bottle cork popping, a fiddle in a can. The saxophone, for a hot minute, was the hip instrument everyone wanted to play—advertisements of the day promised it would make the player the life of the party. It was the equivalent of buying a guitar just to learn how to play "Stairway to Heaven." Making a saxophone "moan" was the 1915 equivalent of your friend, Joe, ruining the party by plugging in his Stratocaster and bleating out a fuzzy rendition

[3]Stephen Cottrell, *The Saxophone* (New Haven: Yale University Press, 2013), 165.

[4]Liane Hansen, "Saxophone's History as 'The Devil's Horn,'" NPR, November 6, 2005, accessed June 24, 2024, https://www.npr.org/templates/story/story.php?storyId=4991482.

of "Sweet Home Alabama." This was what the saxophone was in the early 1900s.

Bless their hearts.

Wiedoeft may have been a walking contradiction, but history does not remember him as a comedian, or one of Tom Brown's clown-faced brothers—though Wiedoeft did things like name his songs "Saxophobia" and "Sax-O-Pun," his influence in bringing the saxophone into the realm of *serious music* is palpable. In 1928, after graduating with a terrifically useful degree in philosophy from Yale, a young musician named Hubert Prior Vallée was so starstruck by Rudy Wiedoeft that he changed his name, forever known from then on as Rudy Vallée.

As we've already discovered, the saxophone is not kind to its greatest champions. Even Wiedoeft, in all his success, didn't get out of life as a sax player without becoming an alcoholic, losing all his money in a Death Valley gold mine (which he mined himself once he could no longer afford workers), getting stabbed by his wife for not keeping her in the lavish lifestyle for which she was accustomed, before succumbing to cirrhosis of the liver in 1940.

Despite his strange decline, Rudy Wiedoeft was a key player in lifting the saxophone out of its lowbrow status, and he cleared the path for the future saxophone virtuoso, the artist behind the instrument, the complex and often troubled individual with addictive personalities—and none of them clowns.

PART II

ON THE MARGINS

4 IMPROVISATION

The term "jazz" has an interesting history, and a scandalous one, depending on what theory tickles your fancy. Originating from the word "jass," likely from African American oral culture, the word itself is said to be related to sex. Or it's from the word "jasmine," a perfume scent commonly used in the Storyville district days of New Orleans, or maybe it's derived from the biblical word "Jezebel," a term meaning *morally unrestrained woman*. One could see how this might present a problem for those concerned with the state of their souls and alignment with conservative morality. Throw in the casual racism popular during that era, the general "racy" lifestyle of the roaring twenties, and *bam*, jazz was a four-letter word. The saxophone, of course, got swept up in the connotations of a style of music that dared to explore sound, rhythm, and syncopation.

I like to think jazz was born on the streets of Storyville, New Orleans, materialized from the humid mist over the Mississippi River, in the fragrant air smelling of perfume, gumbo, cheap whiskey, and the youthful enthusiasm for a good time. But jazz wasn't necessarily born here—it was born in New Orleans, which was a lot more than the ten square blocks that held the red-light district. The red-light district filled with brothels and dance clubs offered a welcoming space for the musicians to play and get paid, being more in the sex business than the music business (and the patrons were less scrutinizing of the music, giving the musicians the freedom to experiment). Jazz fit in here like a long, slender glove. Pianists were called "professors" and blues singers—men and women—lit up the district with iterations of popular ragtime and Tin Pan Alley songs. Musicians like Jelly Roll Morton and Sidney Bechet cut their teeth in the brothels and saloons of Storyville. But Sidney Bechet's claim to the early jazz days of the saxophone wouldn't come until much later, after he'd left New Orleans.

The truth is that the saxophone had little to do with the beginnings of jazz. In the early twentieth century, Buddy Bolden had set the stage for "the trance" that became jazz, blaring his cornet at an impressive volume as he disappeared into unknown territory—improvisation—where "nothing mattered but the music."[1]

So how did the saxophone become the icon of jazz—and not the cornet? Even Joe "King" Oliver and His Creole Jazz Band, an early jazz ensemble, featured two cornets (one of them played by Louis Armstrong). Of course, the cornet

---

[1] "Buddy Bolden," *New Orleans*, n.d., accessed June 15, 2024, https://www .neworleans.com/things-to-do/music/history-and-traditions/buddy -bolden/.

would play a part in shaping the way future sax players would make a name for themselves, the two instruments complementing one another.

In the early 1920s, around the time Buddy Bolden was living out his second decade as a resident in a mental institution—where he would spend nearly twenty-five years at the Louisiana State Insane Asylum for what is now thought to be schizophrenia, though recent theories suggest he might have suffered from pellagra, a serious vitamin deficiency that affected poor Black populations in the South the same year Bolden was committed—Sidney Bechet was handed a soprano saxophone in London.

Bechet discovered the loud, bold, customizable sound the sax offered, and he liked what he heard. He brought the clarinet's vibrato to the soprano, finding such great volume and power in this instrument that he often overpowered the trumpets onstage. In the early 1920s, he played and recorded with Louis Armstrong, the duo helping to bring jazz and swing together. Bechet is long remembered as a soprano mastermind, a pioneer of the saxophone in jazz, and despite his long tenure in Paris (where he died in 1959), he is often remembered as one of the kings of jazz in New Orleans, the Creole musician born to use his troubled mind to bring improvisation to the stage. If the legend and mystery of Buddy Bolden is to be believed, you might say jazz was born in much the same way as the saxophone itself: from trouble, suffering, and ambition that burned so bright it torched everything in its path. It made sense the two should merge.

It's important to note, again, that the saxophone had a moment in the spotlight. It was *the* in-demand instrument of the era of excess, of frivolity, of flappers and flagpole sitting, of prohibition cocktails and smoke-filled dance clubs. There are theories that Sidney Bechet traded his clarinet for a soprano because it was the thing to do that paid the bills. Another theory: it was the devilish sway and charm of the saxophone that appealed to early jazz musicians. The gifts of the saxophone to its formative players were that it gave them the power of individual sound and creativity, sonorous volume, and the undeniable ability to be the center of attention that the soloist craves.

1920s saxophone soloists like Frankie Trumbauer on the C-melody, bass sax player Adrian Rollini, and alto player Jimmy Dorsey, all can be named as major influencers on the saxophone's place in jazz, with admirers such as Lester Young and Coleman Hawkins following their lead (though they'd both eschew the C-melody in favor of the tenor). The domino effect of the saxophone's popularity was palpable— young players picked up the instrument because they wanted to be part of something big, to have a unique voice that no one could replicate, and the sax gave them that gift. You didn't have to know how to read music to make it sing, to make it yours.

Of course, jazz was not relegated to New Orleans. The best of it might have stayed there had the southern states been more welcoming. In fact, there are as many theories about the origins of jazz as there are fish in the sea, with some claiming jazz was born in California, Chicago, New York, Africa, and

Europe, its roots born of ragtime and blues. It is up to the reader to sift through the minutiae of what is legend and what is truth, or at least, what is the truest to them in their search for understanding. As far as I can tell, it's all of the above. The volumes on jazz are immense and overwhelming (and far more thorough than I could ever be), but the takeaway is the saxophone found itself in a tug-of-war with comedy and serious music, slowly inching its way past the clowns, the woodwind sections of the big band ensembles, toward the front and center of the stage.

Coleman Hawkins wasn't the first jazz saxophonist (and was likely influenced by early players such as Stump Evans, Happy Caldwell, and Prince Robertson), but he was the first one to be taken seriously. Born in Missouri in 1904, Hawkins learned how to play piano and cello as a child, giving him a firm grasp on theory and classical music. He is rumored to have cut his teeth on the C-melody sax, but gave it up for the tenor sax, the instrument that would make him a household name. The C-melody fell out of popularity, largely due to its limited range and association with novelty entertainment. It was the sacrificial lamb of sorts, losing favor so that the tenor could become the symbol of jazz. And Coleman Hawkins took it to the top, billed as "Saxophone Boy" for Mamie Smith's Original Jazz Hounds at the age of eighteen.[2] Hawkins moved

---

[2]Richard Havers, "Coleman Hawkins," *uDiscoverMusic*, 2020, accessed February 14, 2020, https://www.udiscovermusic.com/artist/coleman-hawkins/.

to Harlem, New York, in 1922, where many jazz musicians were experimenting with new harmonies and innovations. New York jazz developed after it had already made a mark on New Orleans and migrated to Chicago. Hawkins led the way for the sax to become more than an improvisational tool, but a huge part of the swing era. Hawkins' sound was warm, welcoming, and showcased the range that the tenor sax was capable of, recalling his childhood playing the cello (a similar range of the tenor). Like Bechet, he was a fan of using vibrato, but it was his improvisational ballads and careful articulations that took him to the top, and which influenced a cascade of sax players after. In 1939, Hawk recorded his own variation of Johnny Green's "Body and Soul," which became his most notable song, "the greatest of all jazz solos,"[3] influencing countless jazz musicians then and now. Hawkins worked until his death in 1969, having a forty-five-year body of work, the standards for which, "all jazz tenor saxophone solos will forever be judged."[4]

Though bebop and cool jazz came along near the end of Hawkins' career, he held steady, though not making too many waves, unlike his contemporary, Lester Young, later known as "Prez" or "President," a nickname given to him by Billie Holiday. Young made a name for himself in Count Basie's Orchestra in Kansas City, which geographically played

[3]Gary Giddins, *Jazz* (New York: W.W. Norton, 2009), 163.
[4]John Chilton, *The Song of the Hawk: The Life and Recordings of Coleman Hawkins* (Ann Arbor: University of Michigan Press, 1993), 389.

a huge role in taking the swing style of jazz and carving a path for improvisation and bebop in the 1920s and 1930s. Kansas City was an interesting place to be in the early 1930s, suffering much of the same fate as the rest of the country during the Great Depression, yet also prospering due to its cattle industry, wide-open liquor laws, loosey-goosey operating hours for music halls and jazz clubs, providing generous opportunities for musicians to find paying gigs. In a way, Kansas City was Storyville, reprised. Percussionist Jo Jones recalls his arrival to KC, falling in love with the spirited jam sessions that were never-ending, with music in the air twenty-four hours a day. Sax players lined up (if they had proven their salt) for the chance to hop on the bandstand and blow. One night in early 1934, Coleman Hawkins showed up to jam at the Cherry Blossom, where Count Basie worked. He played all night, getting "hung up," unable to oust the other sax players that joined him, including Young, Ben Webster, Herschel Evans, and Herman Walder. Jones was woken up in the middle of the night by Ben Webster, who urged him to come down to the Blossom because Hawkins was playing with his shirt off. "Sure enough, when we got there, Hawkins was in his singlet, taking turns with the Kaycee men. It seems he had run into something he didn't expect. . . . That was how Hawkins got hung up. . . . He kept trying to blow something to beat Ben and Herschel and Lester. When at last he gave up, he got straight in his car and drove to St. Louis. . . . Yes, Hawkins was king until he met those crazy Kansas City tenor men." Of course, it was all in good spirits. The sense of community during this era was welcoming and respectful. "The idea of the jam session then wasn't who could play better than somebody else," said Jones. "It was a matter of contributing something and of experimentation. Jam sessions were our fun, our outlet."[5]

One of Lester Young's greatest gifts to music, besides showing the world what a cool approach to the saxophone can sound like, is that he influenced a young Charlie Parker, who came of age during the Kansas City jazz era, standing outside of the clubs listening to the sax players when he was twelve and too young to go inside. He studied the techniques of Young by listening to recordings of Count Basie when he wasn't lurking outside the clubs.

Parker, later known as "Yardbird" or "Bird," would build on what he learned from Young—much like every jazz saxophone player before, learning from tradition and putting their own sound to it—and in partnering with Dizzy Gillespie and Thelonious Monk, he created a new jazz language known as bebop, characterized by fast tempos and fragmented solos. Parker's slick style on the alto was infectious, demanding an audience's attention, bringing not the tenor, but the alto saxophone, into the spotlight it so deserved. Unfortunately, with his bad reputation for drug and alcohol abuse, Parker would die young, perhaps taking the brief spotlight away from the alto with him as he went. In Parker's wake, Sonny

---

[5]Nat Shapiro and Nat Hentoff, *Hear Me Talkin' to Ya: The Story of Jazz by the Men Who Made It* (New York: Dover, 1955), 292–293.

Stitt carried on the bebop tradition with the baritone and the tenor, along with Julian "Cannonball" Adderley, who shared much of Parker's agility on the alto, helped form the subgenre of bebop—hard bop—that defined the movement during the 1950s–1960s, and into the jazz fusion of the 1970s. Parker's legacy also influenced powerhouses Phil Woods and Sonny Rollins, landing them all with the moniker of "New Bird," though each were (and still are) hugely influential saxophone players in their own right.

The energy of bop made way for cool jazz, piloted by the likes of Miles Davis, who would influence (and play with) John Coltrane, who would take the saxophone to new heights with his gritty sound and obsession with finding his perfect tone. In the 1950s, Coltrane played sax in bands with Dizzy Gillespie, Jonny Hodges, and Earl Bostic. After getting sober in the late 1950s, Coltrane recorded *Kind of Blue* with Davis in 1959, which became the best-selling jazz album of all time. This could be, theoretically, because of its powerhouse compositions by artists at the top of their game, or because it is simply, unequivocally, beautiful.[6]

The saxophone found itself finally able to rest after such strenuous workouts in vaudeville and Kansas City. Once again, the sax was showing the world its myriad

---

[6]Malcolm Jones, "How 'Kind of Blue' became the best-selling jazz album ever," *Newsweek*, January 30, 2009, accessed June 16, 2024, https://www.newsweek.com/how-kind-blue-became-best-selling-jazz-album-ever-77791.

personalities. It could possess someone to move their feet, and equally compel them to sit down for a nice cocktail. You couldn't throw a rock without hitting the bell of a notable sax player in the age of jazz and its myriad subgenres. From Dexter Gordon's cool tone to Stan Getz's breezy solos, to the controversial (self-taught) free jazz of Ornette Coleman that landed him a Pulitzer, the saxophone's vast and powerful lineage has become the symbol of jazz itself, an extension of the player's soul and personal expression, an exploration of sound as art, and a way to be free during a time that did not give freedom in equal measure.

I could write hundreds of pages about the saxophone's place in jazz, but it would defeat the purpose of this volume. Do not let my adoration of jazz saxophone muddy the truth—many people did not like jazz, and many did not like the saxophone, despite its popularity; critics like Rudi Blesh thought it was disruptive, an unwelcome invader, that "for even an inferior trombone breathes new life into the music which the fashionable foghorn, the saxophone, had murdered."[7] This is a theme that is not unfamiliar to the saxophone, as we've seen from the days of Adolphe Sax. One can only muse what a delight he would have found in the saxophone's popularity (and blatant disregard for the rules) in the jazz age.

But dear reader, I do not think that is why we are here. Charlie Parker said it best, when asked to describe jazz:

---

[7] Rudi Blesh, *Shining Trumpets* (New York: Alfred A. Knopf, 1946), 233.

"Music is your own experience, your thoughts, your wisdom. If you don't live it, it won't come out of your horn. They teach you there's a boundary to music. But, man, there's no boundary line to art."[8]

---

[8]Nat Shapiro and Nat Hentoff, *Hear Me Talkin' to Ya: The Story of Jazz by the Men Who Made It* (New York: Dover, 1955), 405.

SHEET MUSIC #2: NO MORE WEDDINGS, NO MORE FUNERALS

"When we all get to heaven, I know one thing for sure," my dad said, shifting back and forth on his dress shoes. I liked watching the way they dug into the thick red carpet of the church pulpit. "We're gonna have a *large* time." This usually got a few head nods and *Amen!*'s from the congregation. He'd drum the keypads of his tenor, nod his head like a metronome as he waited for the next track to play and launch into a bebop rendition of "When We All Get to Heaven."

He'd started this particular bit of banter not long after his grandmother, Clara, died from emphysema complications in 1994. She'd raised him for much of his childhood. I only knew Grandmother for eight years, but she was in my top three rankings of people I loved and respected. Each Sunday after church, my dad and I would go to her house for lunch.

Grandmother smoked like a power plant, hated the color yellow with a flaming passion, watched "Jeopardy!" daily, had retired from running her own co-op, and always put ketchup and a tub of Country Crock butter next to my plate because she knew how much I loved condiments. She never made me feel bad about my weight, or how much I loved to eat. I was just like my dad. I looked like him, I cracked the same jokes, and I was a fat kid. She called me his "shadow." I wanted nothing more.

After Clara died, my father's music changed. He devoted himself deeply to the church, writing songs and performing covers of hymnals and gospel songs themed around going to heaven. Of course, I knew nothing of thematics as a kid. I heard him practicing these songs every day. I hummed them while I played with my Barbies in the bathroom sink, or while I was picking a switch, stripped of its leaves, from outside to bring back to my mother to receive punishment for mouthing off. His songs about heaven, to me, were a soothing balm against what I was learning about the world. Turns out that's how it worked out for everyone in the church, too, when they heard his tenor wailing out "Holy, Holy, Holy," or "Amazing Grace." The saxophone had spoken to them in church, and just like when Brother B. preached on topics like sin or honoring thy neighbor, they listened. I'd watch them watching him. Some people were so moved by the sax, they'd start crying, or raise their hands high in the air, pumping their palms toward the enormous wooden cross above the baptismal tub built into the wall.

Just like the sermons, my dad's church concerts had a formula. I memorized it.

The congregation filed in, chattered, and I took my place with my sister and mother a few rows toward the front. Armed with the mother-approved small notepad and Crayola markers to keep my fidgety hands to myself, I'd narrow my eyes and listen for the inevitable as my dad set his soprano on its stand, next to the iconic tenor:

"Is that a saxophone?" A woman's voice, sometime a man's, would question loudly to her partner or child. Then they'd point a finger at the soprano. "AND he's going to play a gold clarinet!"

"Actually—" I'd begin to correct them.

My mother shot me a look every time this happened, her lips pressed tight. *Mollie Griffin Hawkins. Don't you dare.*

The preacher would start the service with a prayer. The congregation knew they were in for a treat when they saw the triple instrument stand parked next to the pulpit. The soprano, tenor, and alto saxophones blindingly gold and holy under the fluorescent lighting. The preacher would introduce my dad, who always looked to the ground or smiled, like he was embarrassed to have anyone say anything nice about him. He'd wear black or dark gray slacks, a tucked-in white or light blue starched shirt under a tweed blazer, a wide tie pinned to his shirt with a tie tack. If it were a Sunday or Wednesday evening service, he'd wear one of his "fun" ties, printed with cartoon saxophones or music notes. He was insecure about losing his hair, but he was too respectful to wear one of his nicer pageboy hats inside a church, but his remaining hair was trimmed and his beard tidy. The preacher would leave the stage and take a seat in the front pew. My dad would nod to the sound guys, thumbs up or thumbs down for the levels, and then he'd blow the roof off with his saxophone bebop renditions of classic hymns and *secular* Christian music, which never failed to raise a few eyebrows in rural Alabama.

He played a song or two before launching into witty banter, giving a forty-five-minute set. Instead of an encore, he'd say a prayer to close out. Often, he'd get a standing ovation. He really tooted that horn for the Lord and held those notes like nobody's business. The preacher would come up, say yet another prayer, and then send around a friendly collection plate—the Lord's equivalent of a tip jar. I'd watch the shallow brass bowl (always brass), lined in red velvet (always red velvet), get passed from hand to hand, folded checks and small envelopes being tossed in as it crowd-surfed the pews. At best, he pulled down a couple hundred bucks, which wasn't bad, I thought as a kid, for something he'd be doing for fun anyway.

That's how he ended up as the headliner for countless weddings and funerals.

There was something about the saxophone, or the way my dad played it, that struck a chord with people. Call it nostalgia. Call it belief that the saxophone is a biblical symbol of freedom from oppression, of victory. Or a symbol of being plumb lazy because so-and-so waited until the last minute to get a musical element booked for their daughter's wedding ceremony. Either way, my dad made a name for himself in the church music world. He was local-famous. His songs were played on the Birmingham radio stations. He won contests and went on *The 700 Club*. Twice. Had he been allowed to play real gigs in venues other than churches, who knows where his career could have gone in the 1990s. Instead, he became the local favorite for weddings and funerals.

And it's not like he was the kind of musician that turned down gigs.

My father's saxophones mesmerized the people of Pell City. Usually, people with that kind of talent and education left town immediately. He lacked the self-confidence, and he had a family. And bills. So, we stayed put, in our little brick house, until it was foreclosed on in 2014, a year after I moved to California. But in the 1990s through the early aughts, my dad spent many of his weekends toting one of his horns to a church or a funeral home, to mourn or to celebrate. He never complained. He was honored to be asked. I don't remember what songs he'd play, but this could also be because I wasn't ever invited to the weddings. I would have gone without question, because I would have been happy enough to accompany my dad to the bank to deposit a check, fill the gas tank, or to ship one of many frequent QVC return boxes at the shipping annex. And I loved wedding cake.

At the funerals, though, his number one request was "Danny Boy," a classic Irish song written in 1910 about life, love, and being reunited with those we've lost in death. It was the last track on my dad's 1995 album, *Heaven*. "Danny Boy" is a popular funeral song. Elvis claimed it to be written by angels and wanted it played at his own funeral. Johnny Cash recorded it twice, once at the start of his career—changing the lyrics to third person so that it was a loved ones' grave he'd visit, not his own—and then again in 2002, keeping the original lyrics so that he would be singing of his own death. He died less than a year after recording.

Playing the saxophone at funerals wore my father down. Sometimes, I'd hear him talking to my mother, his voice low and serious. "I wish people would stop asking me to do these," he confessed. "It's tough."

He was too nice to say no. It wasn't just that it was the polite thing to do, it's as though he felt his saxophone bore him a sense of duty, and he was bound to it for life. He enjoyed playing at weddings of people he knew (which was nearly the whole town), but that, too, grew tiring. I think he started to see the ways in which his instrument of choice had become a beacon for the important moments of our lives, and our deaths. And he didn't like having that much say.

The saxophone is the instrument most capable of sounding like the human voice. That's why it was the darling of vaudeville acts as a novelty instrument; it could laugh, moan, and weep. It could take you up and bring you down. Jazz soloists made it the cool leading vocalist for an entire genre of music. It was capable of chaos, of control. It was too happy, it was too sad.

The wedding requests for my dad to play saxophone petered out over time. The funeral requests did not.

5 OBSESSION

The saxophone had a stronghold on early twentieth century entertainment. It also had a grip on its players, as though it fused with their personalities. The saxophone gave them a voice, like it had Adolphe Sax, but it also seemed to give them a curse.

It's not surprising to anyone that a musician might struggle with some of life's saddest afflictions, from addiction to poverty. Jazz and musicians, especially so. The number of musicians that achieved astronomical success and died in poverty, or of addiction-related maladies, is staggering. Many died due to the consequences of excessive alcohol consumption. Charlie Parker (34), Coleman Hawkins (64), Rudy Wiedoeft (49), John Coltrane (41), Stan Getz at (64), and Lester Young (49), for example, all died well below the respective average male lifespan ranging from 60 years old in 1940 to 70+ years old by the end of the century.[1]

---

[1] "Life Expectancy for Social Security," Social Security Administration, 2001, accessed June 16, 2024, https://www.ssa.gov/OACT/TR/TR02/lr5A3-h .html.

In a study conducted by the National Library of Medicine, the author says the lifestyle and pressures jazz musicians face leads to premature deaths, citing eighty musicians that died young, with an estimated 461 years' worth of music we lost with them.[2]

Charlie Parker helped solidify the voice of jazz with his saxophone, but he also used it as currency to pay for his vices. He regularly pawned it to pay for his drug habits. Parker was a tremendous sax player, but his inner demons wreaked havoc, making him a risky booking for the jazz clubs. Birdland, a jazz club in New York City named in honor of Parker, stopped booking him because of his unreliability.

Eventually, Parker's habits caught up to him and he died at age 34, though coroner reports mistakenly assumed he was a man in his 1950s or 1960s. He had four failed marriages, multiple suicide attempts, and mental illness that sent him to prison and then Camarillo State Hospital. The single consistent relationship Parker had was with the saxophone, though it was just as intense.

Parker's contemporaries faced much of the same fate, begging the question—did the saxophone help or hurt their lives? Their success as musicians led them to lead difficult lives, but would they have experienced the same fates otherwise? After all, American healthcare has never

---

[2]Keith Rayner, et al., "The lost years: The impact of cirrhosis on the history of jazz," National Center for Biotechnology Information, September 2001, https://www.ncbi.nlm.nih.gov/pmc/articles/PMC2721805/.

been favorable or generous, and those who need it most are often denied or driven into medical debt. And that is if they seek care at all. The stigma associated with getting mental healthcare is very real to this day.

Despite jazz being declared a national treasure by the United States Congress in 1987, it means didley squat when the United States does little to fund the arts or its artists. According to a 2003 study by Joan Jeffri for the National Endowment for the Arts (NEA), a mere 63.3 percent of 700+ surveyed jazz musicians had health or medical coverage, far lower than the national average of 87 percent.[3] These numbers haven't improved in the past couple of decades. Since many Americans have health insurance through steady employment, full-time musicians don't have this luxury. With premiums also being often out of reach, it's easy to avoid seeking care because the fees are not transparent. Added to that, there are racial disparities and accessibility issues for many minority groups in this country—it's no wonder why so many musicians try to avoid it altogether until it's too late. Considering many of the sax players in the early- to mid-jazz era were Black or African American, existing in a tumultuous time for civil rights was a war within itself. The saxophone seemed to only encourage a war within themselves, too, but the irreplaceable music they

---

[3] Joan Jeffri, "Changing the Beat: A Study of the Worklife of Jazz Musicians." National Endowment for the Arts, 2003, accessed December 9, 2023, https://www.arts.gov/impact/research/publications/changing-beat-study-worklife-jazz-musicians.

gave to us evolved into a national treasure (though one we seem to rarely encourage in monetary ways).

After getting sober, the effects of substance abuse made a permanent mark on Coltrane, regardless of good intentions. Though John Coltrane got clean and experienced a profound spiritual awakening in the process, the damage to his body was already done; he'd die from liver cancer at only forty years old, likely encouraged by hepatitis from his needle use days. Stan Getz suffered the same fate, though not until he was sixty-four. Getz, too, tried to free himself from the grips of addiction, moving his family to Denmark, in part to place distance between the pressures of American drug culture. Upon his death in 1991, Getz was cremated, and his ashes were poured from his saxophone case off the coast of Marina Del Ray in California.

Imagine being so obsessed with the object that made you *who* you are, that your body and soul fuses within the space it contains. You become the extension of the saxophone's eternal soul, not the other way around.

Fame is a double-edged sword. Musicians burn bright and sometimes die young, or middle-aged by the delayed effects of heavy substance abuse. Researching the lists of saxophone players that were claimed early, a word comes up often: destitute. Adolphe Sax was the first in a long line of musicians tormented by the effects of the saxophone, dying penniless after a life spent in total devotion their one true love, the engine propelling them forward—the saxophone.

Like my father said, once the saxophone is your obsession, that's it. That's your fate drawn out like a red carpet, likely leading nowhere lucrative. Nowhere safe. But out of this, comes jazz, meaning, freedom of expression, and the human experience.

It's as though the saxophone is just as addictive as alcohol or drugs, and one will do *whatever* it takes to keep playing. After all, Bird always managed to get his saxophone out of hock. So did my father. There is always another song to be played to replace the last.

SHEET MUSIC #3: CALL AND RESPONSE

My dad did not have health insurance and hadn't for decades. He worked six days a week for a church that used a legal loophole allowing them not to pay overtime or benefits of any kind. If you ask me, it seems counterintuitive to what they stand for, but my dad put up with it because "no one else will hire an old man." He wrecked his knees working physical labor in the summers when there were no students to teach how to play instruments. He taught history and math, or whatever class needed a teacher. Anything the church wanted him to do, he did it, because the church offered him something he could not get elsewhere: an open and free place to practice saxophone. He couldn't practice saxophone in his apartment in Sacramento. Neighbors complained about dog barks, who knows what they would have done about daily saxophone practice.

He didn't complain, because he was happy to be working on a new Christmas album of bebop covers. It came out two months before he caught Covid, which was around the same time he'd become eligible for Medicare. He waited too long to go to the doctor, which led to a late-night ambulance. Before this, I only remember him going to the doctor once, when I was five or six-years-old, to remove a sinister mole on his neck that turned out benign. He was not a go-to-the-doctor kind of person, of the generation that believed anything could be walked, slept, or starved off. He didn't know anyone that had died from Covid. He'd be fine. He went to work and he came home.

This was the end of 2021, when Covid was "simmering down." He was not vaccinated. Despite begging him to do it (though not hard enough?), he treated the vaccine with the nonchalance of someone too busy to care about himself. "Don't worry about me, worry about you," was one of the last things he said to me. "I'll be okay." And every time he'd said those words to me before, throughout my life, I believed him because he was always right. He was above sickness because no one else was going to pay the bills, cook the meals, and walk the dog. He was not thinking about the bigger picture, or the implications on himself or others.

Here's the truth I want to believe: he didn't get vaccinated because he had no time. He couldn't afford to miss work if the vaccine knocked him off his feet for a few days.

And here's the truth I don't want to believe: my dad was terrified of needles. He never got shots. He was on the wrong side of things entirely. At my wedding reception dinner in New Orleans six months before he caught Covid, he defended the idea that people might be nervous to get the vaccine because of what happened to children in 1955 when 40,000 children contracted polio from a botched vaccine from Cutter Laboratories, 200 suffered paralysis, and 10 died.[1]

What fewer people talk about is that after Cutter fixed the error, people jumped back in line to get their children vaccinated, because the danger of polio was far greater than the danger of a vaccine. In the week my father died, nearly 49,000 other people in the world also lost their lives to Covid.[2] In *one* week.

Somewhere in there is a truth only he knows.

I tell this to the ICU nurses taking care of him in his last days. I apologize for him; I explain how we are not like that. I begged him to get vaccinated. He was just stubborn, busy, but he's a talented musician and there's *no way* his lungs aren't made of steel. How could they be in organ failure? To my horror, the nurses and jaded, curt doctor didn't seem to believe me as I enunciated my words through two layers of masks and a plastic face shield: *my father is a real, good, kind person. He's been playing the saxophone for hours every day*

---

[1] Rae Ellen Bichell, "Can't Help Falling in Love With a Vaccine: How Polio Campaign Beat Vaccine Hesitancy," NPR, May 3, 2021, accessed December 8, 2023, https://www.npr.org/sections/health-shots/2021/05/03/988756973 /cant-help-falling-in-love-with-a-vaccine-how-polio-campaign-beat -vaccine-hesitan505007/.

[2] "COVID-19 Dashboard: Deaths," World Health Organization, 2024, https://data.who.int/dashboards/covid19/deaths?n=c.

since he was in the fifth grade. He works so hard. He did not mean for this to happen. He would be so ashamed.

It's easy to fall into the trap of thinking that just because someone is talented, and loved by many people, they'll be around forever. There's something about saxophone players that feels like they are of a mettle the rest of us are not, that they are full of a fire that breathes out art, and therefore they are immortal. The saxophone pulled them in with a promise, but the problem is it doesn't always deliver the way we'd hope.

In the ICU, all I wanted was for the staff to understand how incredible my father was, and not to treat him poorly because he was on Medicare. I overstayed my one-hour-per-day visiting limit, and they let me. Because when the rules don't apply to you, nothing good is going to happen. So I put on layers of PPE and sat in the small, cold room crowded with buzzing and beeping machines and endless tangles of IV drips, and I played my father jazz—everything I could think of with a saxophone—from a playlist I made on my phone on the flight to Sacramento. I played it at full volume and put in close to his ear because he was hard of hearing after never wearing earplugs. The ICU staff glanced into the wall of clear plexiglass, but never complained about the noise. I played him jazz on my phone and then left the little corner television station on a jazz music channel. It was Muzak, at best, but it was better than silence. Is there anything worse for a musician than being trapped in a room filled only with the sonorous drone of machines?

It was all fast, and frenetic, and I could not slow it down to study it like a song, or remember the right things to say in a prayer, or appeal to whatever gods had an ear tilted toward this shadowy place.

I watched a documentary recently called *The Devil's Horn,* based on the book of the same title, which examines the validity of whether the saxophone is "evil." The documentary features a handful of sax players, including a New York City saxophone jazz legend that mysteriously disappeared for decades, Giuseppe Logan. Before landing in a nursing facility, he was homeless, haunted by a life of drug abuse and a criminal record. He found solace and comfort when playing his sax in Tompkins Square Park. By the time the camera crews showed up, he'd lost all his teeth, but he could still play the loner horn that a local musician and shop worker gave to him. Even in the end, at the nursing home, he struggles to breathe life into the saxophone, but he does it. That's the power of this instrument. It isn't something you can retire. I thought about this often, what would my father do with himself when he was too old and feeble to play a saxophone? In the hospital, I thought, what kind of recovery will this be if he can't play his saxophone for a while? What kind of life can you have when you can't do the *one* thing in this world that makes you happy?

In hindsight, I explore dark corners of thought about my dad's last week in the ICU. Greg, intubated and prone, with machines throwing warnings and exclamation points the staff shrugged off, some talking to me like I should be ashamed of the situation, the doctor seeming to know the day and hour in which my father would die. Just before his lunch break at noon on Saturday, December 18. They were tired of dealing with me, and my sister's attempts to get him transferred to another hospital after discovering this one didn't have *any* Covid survivors. They seemed to have them on two-week timers—and it all doesn't leave me feeling very settled. But again, 10,000 people died of the same thing the week before Christmas. We aren't special. In the end, we're all numbers on someone's Excel spreadsheet. One of my writing teachers will say, in a lecture, "no one's death is a tragedy," and I think about that every day.

Giuseppe Logan died of Covid in 2020. Other sax players, Lee Konitz, Marcelo Peralta, Manu Dibango, followed suit. Of course, the other side of this is maybe that's when their card came up. There are no guarantees in life, and more so with Covid. Vaccinated people died, too. It seemed arbitrary, how many people it would take and how many it would leave—and some with lasting effects of which we still don't know much about. Some people got lucky. Steve Barlotta, a saxophonist in New Jersey who has played with Bruce Springsteen, the Monkees, and Jon Bon Jovi, was 59 when he caught Covid. He was on a ventilator for a month but came out of it able to move nothing but his thumb.[3] After months

---

[3]Jerry Carino, "'Highlight of my career': Saxophonist who survived COVID plays for hospital that saved him," *Asbury Park Press*, September 16, 2022, accessed December 9, 2023, https://www.app.com/story/news/health/2022/09/16/centrastate-hospital-covid-patient-saxophone-concert-thank-you/69491505007/.

of rehab, he was well enough to play a 90-minute concert outside of the hospital where he received care, as a thank you to the staff.

Am I a bad person because it makes me angry my dad didn't get that chance? Or furious that people on the margins of poverty don't often receive gentle care (if any)? Dad was poor. He was unvaccinated. There was no way he could pay for rehab. How many other musicians have faced the same fate, not just now, but since the beginning of jazz? His doctor stopped care after a week in the ICU. On day two or three into my daily visits, the tall, blonde doctor said with no warmth, "Your father *is* going to die."

I'm sure there are thousands of people that heard those same words, in that exact scenario, the past few years. Especially in America's for-profit healthcare industries, where children might beg the staff to treat a parent like a person that deserves the chance to live, so that they can put more beauty into the world. But the world we live in— sometimes it feels like the music, and its history, just keeps getting quieter and quieter.

6 SEDUCTION

"I can't trust myself. I have this thing about saxophone players. Especially tenor sax. I don't know what it is, they just curdle me. All they have to do is play eight bars of 'Come to Me, My Melancholy Baby' and my spine turns to custard, and I get goose-pimply all over—and I come to 'em."

—MARILYN MONROE, *SOME LIKE IT HOT* (1959)

The saxophone was banned from early Hollywood movie scores because it was considered leud, a symbol of sexuality and immoral behavior. The Legion of Decency, an organization run by the Catholic church from 1934 until 1980, made it their mission to slap ratings on films they deemed unsuitable and offensive. In 1954 they flagged *A Streetcar Named Desire* for several reasons, one being the "lustful and carnal scoring" featuring a saxophone, meant to convey the lust and conflicting emotions Stella feels toward her husband, Stanley. The "C" rating slapped on the film stood for "condemned," causing the film editors to cut the scene in a way that pleased the censors on a second pass, omitting the saxophone's interlude.[1]

In what would undoubtedly delight its inventor, the saxophone had become a louder voice than the church wanted it to be. They weren't alone, seeing as Nazi Germany had also banned it on radio stations for being symbolic of jazz culture—and therefore, African American or Jewish—and thus "degenerate," going so far as to knock the saxophone from a player's mouth if they were caught. So, too, did the Soviet Union ban the sax, arresting or sending its players into exile.[2]

Of course, we all know that high-control groups are no stranger to banning things for arbitrary (see also: racist) reasons, but it's interesting that a piece of brass could rattle so many chains in such a short length of time, for such a small thing to hold such power over threatened men that were evil incarnate and/or catastrophically dangerous.

Could it also be that the saxophone is symbolic of pure sensuality and femininity, despite its players often being

[1] Jonathan Rhodes Lee, "Original Soundtrack from 'A Streetcar Named Desire,'" National Registry, 2015, accessed December 8, 2023, https://www.loc.gov/static/programs/national-recording-preservation-board/documents/Streetcar-Named-Desire-Soundtrack_Lee.pdf.

[2] "Saxophone: History of the Musical Instrument That's Both Brutal and Beautiful," ABC News, February 25, 2020, https://www.abc.net.au/news/2020-02-25/saxophone-history-of-musical-instrument-brutal-and-beautiful/11960922.

male? Its shape is serpentine, sure, but one can easily imagine it as the curvy shape of a woman. The player is ostensibly in control of the instrument, but is it the other way around? History suggests it could be true.

By the 1970s, the saxophone began cross-pollinating into other genres of music, carving out a place for itself in pop, rock and soft rock, and R&B, joining bands as though it were a backup vocalist often stealing the show. By then, an ironclad theme had emerged in which the saxophone was synonymous with love and deep wanting. In 1977, Billy Joel recorded "Just the Way You Are" with Phil Woods, in which his alto sax croons alongside Joel's vocals like butter. A year later came the song that popularized the saxophone solo, Gerry Rafferty's "Baker Street," a man wishes to own a home and cannot reach his goal because he's an alcoholic. Raphael Ravenscroft played the famous eight-bar alto solo that to this day remains one of the most iconic songs in music history.

In 1984, George Michael released "Careless Whisper," about a man's guilt over an illicit affair. Steve Gregory's alto solo brings the listener into a lush, rich world as Michael sings woefully about sleazing around.

Sade, an English band led by Sade Adu, released their genre-bending pop-jazz-R&B second album, *Promise*, in 1985. Woven throughout the album is the saxophone accompaniment of Stuart Matthewman, who made quite the impact on the band's successful debut, *Diamond Life,* the year prior. In "Jezebel," Sade's soulful voice tells the story of a woman who must fight for everything she has, though it might make her unpopular. Perhaps drawing on the classic biblical story of Jezebel, the saxophone's place in the song acts as the seductive siren that amplifies Jezebel's femininity and power.

Critics hated *Promise*. In a *Rolling Stone* review, the critic downplayed Sade's talents, likening her sultry voice to wallpaper, that "the careful elegance of the production and instrumental settings seems little more than a strategy to conceal the limitations of Sade's vocal range."[3] However, *Promise* was a huge commercial success, landing the band a #1 spot on the US Billboard 200. If it wasn't Sade's silky vocals resonating with listeners—could it have been Matthewman's seductive saxophone vocals, instead, speaking directly into the ears of the eager audience?

By the end of the 1980s, the saxophone had become not only a voice of jazz, but also one capable of enchanting and casting a spell on its listener. And who can explain love in any way that makes tangible sense? Certainly not a critic. Rudi Blesh, the jazz historian, and critic of the early- to mid-twentieth century (you know—the guy that thought of the sax as a fashionable foghorn), claiming there was no place for love in jazz, either: "Jazz is a lean and athletic music,

---

[3]Anthony DeCurtis, "Sade: Promise," *Rolling Stone*, January 30, 1986, accessed December 16, 2023 via the Wayback Machine, https://web.archive .org/web/20090630030145/http://www.rollingstone.com/artists/sade/ albums/album/208219/review/5946308/promise.

unobsessed with romantic or commercial love," he claims. "It shuns sentimentality and the languors of romantic desire."[4]

So how did we get here, with the saxophone leading us into the world of love ballads? Was the saxophone the best friend that we were in love with all along? The problem is that many of the pop songs of the 80's featured the man who slicked back his hair and sang about love.

The argument can be made that the "Careless Whisper" effect opened the door for parody, recalling the saxophone's past life as a novelty, or comedy, instrument. The difference is that the leader was no longer wearing a clown suit, but instead a tank top and slicked-back hair, a corny symbol of the "sexy sax guy" or as a punchline of a joke featuring the "greasy 80's man."[5] The saxophone is always guilty by association.

Even today, the saxophone is a symbol of comedic lust; one needs only watch any episode of *Scrubs* (2001–2010) to understand the lustful feelings of JD, cued by the same saxophone interlude and soft camera focus on whatever female he had his sights on. The saxophone is Pavlov and we are its horny animals.

A *Forbes* article from April 2023 reveals that "Careless Whisper" is one of only eight songs from the 1980s to hit over one billion views on YouTube (and climbing), though

---

[4] Rudi Blesh, *Shining Trumpets* (Alfred A. Knopf, 1946), 200.
[5] Kelsey McKinney, "Where Did All the Saxophones Go?," *The Outline*, April 25, 2017, accessed December 15, 2023, https://theoutline.com/post/1409/saxophones-in-american-pop-music-history.

they can't quite put their finger on the "x-factor" that makes the song so memorable, so charming, that people return to it again and again.[6]

But any casual saxophone fan could tell you exactly why.

---

[6]Peter Suciu, "Shhh! George Michael's 1984 Hit 'Careless Whisper' Has Just Racked Up A Billion Views On YouTube," *Forbes*, April 2023, accessed December 15, 2023, https://www.forbes.com/sites/petersuciu/2023/04/03 /shhh-george-michaels-1984-hit-careless-whisper-has-just-racked-up-a -billion-views-on-youtube/?sh=2f13e1cb5d81.

SHEET MUSIC #4: NUISANCE

For all its charisma, the saxophone draws strong emotions, often landing on two ends of a love/hate spectrum, rarely in-between. It seems to have a cilantro effect; it is bitter, or it is capable of being the star of the meal. And as a Highly Sensitive Person, and kid of a saxophonist, I am quick to snap into defense mode when someone talks trash about the horn. I call it a personal flaw. I call it love.

In a 2007 *AV Club* article titled "Don't Blow It: 10 Great Songs Nearly Ruined By Saxophone," Josh Modell claims the saxophone in pop rock is pure pain, a jolt to the senses, a ruinous additive to popular songs otherwise enjoyable. David Bowie's "Young Americans"; Radiohead's "National Anthem"; The Cure's "A Night Like This," and "Jungleland" by Bruce Springsteen all make the list of offenders. In David Bowie's 1975 recording of "Young Americans," Modell admits, "it'd be easy to argue that the sax actually *makes* 'Young Americans,' but imagine the greatness it could've achieved without the constant nagging and yipping."[1] Throughout his list is the repeated use of the word *bleat*. David Sandborn, the sax player on "Young Americans," would go on to record twenty-four albums (eight of which are gold, one platinum), win six Grammy Awards, and has become one of the most influential and sought-after saxophonists.

It makes sense that people would be irritated by the saxophone in the way one gets fatigued from hearing the same one-hit-wonder on the radio. All those simple, cheesy hooks that left many mouths with sour tastes in the 1980s. The songs with dance moves like the Macarena. Everybody has a song or two that makes their eyes instantly roll toward the ceiling.

But saxophone fatigue isn't my reality. My eyes and throat ache when "Careless Whisper" or "Baker Street" plays in the mall. Don't get me started on "Us and Them." I'll stop short, point at the ceiling. "Such a great song. That's my jam," I'll say, transported right back to the little brick house, my dad's enormous speakers blasting those songs at a volume that rattled the walls.

When you grow up knowing nothing other than living in an environment where a parent plays their multiple saxophones in your house every day, who pays the mortgage

---

[1] Josh Modell, "Don't Blow It: 10 Great Songs Nearly Ruined By Saxophone," *AV Club*, September 10, 2007, accessed December 15, 2023, https://www.avclub.com/dont-blow-it-10-great-songs-nearly-ruined-by-saxophone-1798212377.

with money made from knowing how to teach others to play the saxophone—it's jarring when you are presented with the opinions of people who did *not* grow up that way. As I got older, I noticed the deep sighs of dread, the stirring of controversy, the civic unrest that covered the church congregation like a fog as my father entered the pulpit with a tenor hitched to his neck strap. I watched with rage flaming my fat cheeks as little boys boxed their ears and slid their slinky bodies off the pews dramatically when the first notes of "As the Deer" floated through the air. Adults had similar reactions every now and then, quietly excusing themselves out the back door, their eyes wide and heads shaking, appalled on behalf of Jesus's delicate ears.

It didn't bother my dad. He'd lived his life playing the saxophone whether people liked it or not.

It bothered me, though. I was obsessed with my dad. He could do no wrong; he was talented, the best sax player in the world, the kindest person who loved nothing more than music, southern food, and letting his daughter follow him around like a loyal Chihuahua. He was not perfect, I know that, and we disagreed on many things later. But his music was close to perfect in many ways. And it pissed me off when people acted like it could be anything other than a pure delight.

Sometimes the saxophone sneaks up on me where I least expect. A few months ago, in attempts to forget about the heat wave sizzling over the metro Seattle area, I binge watched *The King of Queens*. There's an episode from 2002 featuring

Eddie Money, of "Two Tickets to Paradise" fame, belting a saxophone solo in the middle of Doug and Carrie's living room. Not three seconds into his solo, do the characters start clapping and say it's time to wrap it up and go. "But why?" I ask the television screen, offended.

The little boys that slid out of their seats, holding their ears as though afraid they'd fall off, they'd end up playing air saxophone by the last song. Once, after a church service concert, one of these boys became so starstruck, he asked his mother for ten dollars to buy a copy of my dad's cassette tape, *Heaven,* and asked my dad to autograph it. I enjoyed watching my father cast a spell with his saxophone, turning the haters into lovers.

And the ones that left the room as he played, well. I imagine they're still miserable, somewhere in rural Alabama, complaining about Music Today as they turn up their televisions.

The nerve!

PART III

A CULT OF PERSONALITY

7 SACRED AND PROFANE

In the Christian tradition, Gabriel's horn is meant to signal Judgement Day, or the second coming of Jesus Christ to condemn sinners and give the righteous a place in heaven. It's easy to imagine the saxophone as a direct descendent of Gabriel's primitive horn, descending from the skies and holding a powerful note, rattling the ribs of billions as it beckons them home.

There are, indeed, those who believe the saxophone's power to be divine—a true mouthpiece for the Lord.

Some go so far as to canonize its players.

When John Coltrane was going through the hellish withdrawal symptoms of heroin and alcohol in 1957, he claimed to have heard the voice of God, which triggered within him a powerful spiritual awakening. The classic album he recorded in 1964, *A Love Supreme,* made evident his devotion to music in the name of a generalized God; Coltrane's interest grew to respect *all* walks of spirituality, intending (it would seem) to simply be a gracious human and use his music to make people happy.

The Saint John Coltrane African Orthodox Church in San Francisco took Coltrane's life work to heart, deifying his music and quotes into a full-blown church experience. Their website is a mix of Coltrane and Dr. Martin Luther King, Jr. quotes about music, love, and social justice. The first Sunday of the month features "A Love Supreme Meditation," where the congregation can be, "guided through a meditation on the testimony and music of Saint John Coltrane's *A Love Supreme*. Great for old time Coltrane lovers and new listeners as well. Join us and experience the power of this anointed sound...the music and wisdom of Saint John Coltrane."[1]

The Saint John Coltrane African Orthodox Church website features paintings of John Coltrane as a true saint, holding up his horn with his left hand, the right gripping a scroll with a prayer emblazoned upon it. The bell of Coltrane's tenor is filled with flames. The church recently celebrated its fiftieth anniversary, commemorated with a party to coincide with "Saint John Will-I-Am Coltrane," the artwork featuring two tenor saxophones illustrated into the shape of a cross.

If you ask the Catholic church, however, they might not agree with worshipping alongside a sinful saxophone. In 1903, Pope Pius X banned the saxophone from the Catholic church because it sounded vulgar, offensive, and prohibited its use

---

[1]"A Love Supreme Meditation," Coltrane Church, accessed June 16, 2024, https://www.coltranechurch.org/.

in sacred music.[2] The saxophone became an easy scapegoat for the frivolity of dance clubs and so-called Bacchanalian behavior of early twentieth century America. In a 1917 *San Francisco Chronicle* article titled "The Saxophone: Siren of Satan," the author demands something be done about this dangerous instrument, that in dance music it "preys upon the passions and emotions. It becomes patently suggestive, instinctly [*sic*] animal-like. No other music instrument can be so immoral. . . ." And goes on to claim the saxophone possesses its listener in a literal sense, rendering them incapable of self-control.[3]

For others, the saxophone is a talisman for equality, beauty, and freedom.

The Saint John Coltrane African Orthodox Church *did* canonize Coltrane as a saint, via the African Orthodox Church, in 1982. Since then the church has been teaching what they call "Coltrane Consciousness." According to an interview with the church organizers, Coltrane's music struck them, "as though he was speaking in tongues and there was fire coming from heaven—a sound baptism," they said.

---

[2]"The Joy of Adolphe Sax: A Major Exhibition Brings Together Rare Saxophones for the First Time Since 1877," *The Independent*, August 15, 2014, accessed December 18, 2023, https://www.independent.co.uk/arts-entertainment/music/features/the-joy-of-adolphe-sax-a-major-exhibition-brings-together-rare-saxophones-for-the-first-time-since-1877-9660320.html.

[3]Isador Berger, "The Saxophone: Siren of Satan," *San Francisco Chronicle*, January 14, 1917.

People travel from across the globe to visit the church in San Francisco, "to attend these services the way other devotees might travel to Rishikesh, India, or Jerusalem."[4]

There is something about losing musicians when they are young, that makes them immortal. Just look at the cultural phenomenon of the "twenty-seven Club," featuring the likes of Kurt Cobain, Janis Joplin, Jimi Hendrix, and Amy Winehouse (to name a few). John Coltrane died at forty of liver cancer, or ten years after his sobriety and spiritual awakening. When musicians die young, their music lives on in perpetuity, casting from it the ability to forever be analyzed, reconfigured to shape a new meaning for modern times, or worshipped. Isn't that what Nirvana fans did upon hearing the news in 1994 that Kurt had died by suicide? Isn't that what all of us do when someone we care about dies? We reminisce. We long. We create gods.

Cobain, another musician to get pulled into the death grips of addiction. When Elliott Smith died in 2003, I was crushed. I listened to his albums on repeat. I was seventeen, a fat girl in rural Alabama, with a generalized anxiety disorder and chronic depression. Smith's lyrics spoke to me the way no one else could—understandable, considering how his own mental illness, depression, and addictions fueled his

---

[4]M.H. Miller, "The Canonization of Saint John Coltrane," *The New York Times Style Magazine*, December 3, 2021, accessed December 18, 2023, https://www.nytimes.com/2021/12/03/t-magazine/john-coltrane-church.html.

lyrics. I suddenly wanted to know everything about his life; who he dated so that I could blame them (as many had blamed Courtney Love); what he believed in besides heroin and sadness. I was obsessed with a person I had never met, but who I'd placed on a pedestal because I related to their sadness and their music transported me to a place wonderful and unreachable to anyone but me.

Seventeen years old or not, it's easy to cast imperfect people in a holy light when they die. Sinners become saints.

Maybe there's something to it, canonizing fallible people that give us beautiful music. After all, the music will outlive us all. If all churches were this great, filled with music and celebration of life, equal rights, and carrying out acts of good faith in the community, perhaps more people attend.

As of this writing, the Vatican's ban on the saxophone has not been lifted.

SHEET MUSIC #5: POINTLESS DEVOTION

A few weeks ago, I did something embarrassing. I looked up the Christian Broadcasting Network (CBN), the media production company of Pat Robertson and *The 700 Club* and clicked on their website. In the past few decades, they've used their platform to stand against things I believe in (equality, women's rights, common sense), but they had something I wanted. So, I found the Contact Us form. And I asked them if they had an archive of a show in 1995, featuring a saxophone player named Greg Hawkins who won a round of the 1995 National New Artist Search. It was *American Idol* before *American Idol*, but for Christians with cable.

I was eight years old when my parents drove thirteen hours in our white Chevy Lumina to Virginia Beach, Virginia, for my dad to play his horn, gain public exposure for his music, and be "launched." I remember nothing about this time other than there were two trips: the first, they went without me and my sister. It snowed in Alabama while they were gone. Somewhere in my grandmother's house there's a photo of my sister and I, grinning wide as we played in the scant inch of snow, socks covering our hands because we didn't have gloves—who needs winter gloves in the Deep South?—and squeezed into layers of sweaters and jackets. It was Super Bowl weekend (though in Alabama, you're hard pressed to find anyone that cares as much about the Super Bowl as they do the Iron Bowl, or Alabama vs. Auburn). Greg won in the preliminary round of artists. The second trip to Virginia Beach, my sister and I got to go with them. It was luxurious.

What I remember is my dad buying us an original Game Boy with two games: Tetris and Yoshi's Cookies. He did this primarily because he wanted his kids not to argue about nonsense in the back seat for thirteen hours, but also because he partook our Super Nintendo as much as we did, and he could play Tetris for hours. So instead, his kids argued in the backseat about whose turn it was on the Game Boy.

We were too young to be part of the taping of *The 700 Club*. My sister is eighteen months older than me, and capable of just as much nonsense. Instead, we stayed in the hotel room—the fanciest place I had ever been in my life, The Founder's Inn, with its beautiful European landscaping and gardens, indoor pool, and fountains with elegant geese gliding through, and a place for which I would measure all future hotels—and my dad recorded the final round of the show. He didn't win. But we won the vacation lottery; we got to walk around a fancy hotel like we belonged there. We saw the beach. We saw historical sites that were both boring and free of charge. We ordered room service.

Less than twenty-four hours after sending my contact form, a representative at CBN replied. They found the footage of my dad, and they sent it to me, no questions asked. The seventeen-minute video shows both segments of my dad playing on the sound stage. The intro music to *The 700 Club* is classic 1990s kitsch, the live band clad in Uncle Jessie's rocker mullet from *Full House*, complete with button-down shirts decked out underneath decorative vests that look like they're made from decorator's fabric. My dad's soprano saxophone shimmers under the studio lights as he plays "Warriors," a song that would become iconic of his style, and often draw people from their seats as he held notes for impossible stretches of time.

What is striking about this video clip is that my dad is *young*. He was thirty-nine, a year older than I am now. He was already balding, but his hair hadn't gone gray yet. He wore a starched dress shirt and a bolo tie. His big smile reached his ocean blue eyes. He was lighter, airier, as though the world hadn't beat on him yet.

Here's the phrases I often told my dad, like a pull-string doll: *Don't let anyone make you think you aren't talented. They don't deserve you. You can do better.* I always believed my dad wasted his talents in churches, when he should have been getting himself out there, playing gigs in *real* venues, having sessions with *real* musicians.

It never occurred to me that he was happy just playing in churches. In fact, the school-church he worked in had become the only place he could practice and record. His YouTube channel features videos he filmed in classrooms, and a couple in a gymnasium. Sometimes he rigged the video with a green screen so that the backgrounds looked like beautiful homes, a fireplace crackling, Christmas decorations strung across a marble mantle. In one video, there's a missing ceiling tile and wires dangling from the ceiling.

I will always wonder, in the same way I wonder about myself, had I stayed in nursing school and not bolted out the door fifteen minutes into the first day of class, or graduated from college earlier, what my father could have done with his life had he not gotten trapped working for church-school-combos. I imagine a life where he stayed as a band director for the public-school systems, and not quit because we moved too far away for his commute. I imagine a life where he had health insurance, benefits, a 401k, and life insurance. A life where he didn't drive beater cars and spend large periods of his later life on the margins of homelessness. And I also wonder: Would money have made a difference? All he wanted were his saxophones and a place to play it like he meant it. His self-proclaimed style: "praise and worship meets hillbilly bebop."

I always thought my dad was at war with his own voice. But he wasn't—he knew exactly what he sounded like, and what he was capable of. The problem is that he didn't think it was worth more than church. More than us.

Another video I find as I'm looking through my dad's email, forever searching for clues to a mystery I can't name: a recording of my dad being interviewed by the pastor's son, in July 2021, five months before he caught Covid from teaching in those same classrooms. For a church service, he plays a handful of songs and then hoists himself up on a chair next to the wooden pulpit, while the pastor's son makes fun of his bad knee. The bad knee he acquired from working manual labor during the summers there. It makes me angry, but Greg laughs it off. He is incapable of holding a grudge, but I recognize the small downtick in his laugh because it's the same one I have when I'm trying not to act like my feelings just got hurt.

During the interview, Greg answers questions about how he started playing in churches. Like a lot of southern country kids, he went to church with his grandparents and spent the service in the back pew with his buddies, "Playing tic-tac-toe," he says to the interviewer. "Because I was like, you know, if heaven is anything like church, I don't know if I want to go. I was bored out of my mind until God got ahold of my heart and changed everything."

When I hear this, I think about faith, and what draws people toward it like a flame. From day one on this earth, I was immersed into an obsessive, oppressive religion as a lifelong ritual. But Dad never talked about it; he just worked in churches. It was a job. He'd been burned by churches, abused, and sent to the poorhouse by the people claiming to be closest to God. As he'll say during the interview, "I'm from a place where, if you mess up in church, you're—" he swipes a hand across his throat. "Toast."

I had tremendous guilt when he died. I felt terrible for not helping him out more. Calling him more. All I did was nag him to find another job, one that didn't make him climb literal, not corporate, ladders, and rip up parking lots. I helped him polish his resume. I texted him job openings. I believed he was amazing, smart, and loyal to a fault; a company would be foolish not to hire him. He could get gigs in the local bars and restaurants; he could make real money. His car often broke down on the side of the freeway on his way to work. He carried gallons of water in the trunk for when it overheated in the punishing California sun. I wish I had the money, myself, to buy him a better car. I was sure he'd get shot on Fulton Avenue one of those times, standing next to his car on the cellphone he got for free from a government program. I wish I had been one of the people he'd called. But he never asked his kids for help. He'd call the church, where somebody always answered. They let him borrow the school's van until he could get his car fixed. In 2021 he was over the moon to get a used 2007 Toyota Corolla. We compared notes because I drove a 2008 Toyota Yaris. We loved our Toyotas because they were hearty, reliable, and reasonably priced. We both had built-in CD players and crank windows.

It's easy for me to be angry at the church, and to not believe in a god that made a kind, gentle person like my father struggle—how any god could allow such suffering in this world. I am a firm believer in science, evolution, and the theory of Occam's razor, that the simplest explanation is often the correct one. It angered me that he spent the better part of his life busying himself in pointless devotions. I watched him stagger through a life often turned away from *church people,* the ones who did nothing when he lost the house to foreclosure, the ones that looked the other way when he was desperately looking for a job. The ones that only came around when they wanted him to play his saxophone at an event. I held hatred for these people for a long time, because it is far easier to be angry than to let things go, or to think that he did all these things by choice. Because who would choose abusive relationships?

The last conversation I have with my dad is over text message while he's in the hospital, a few days before he stopped texting anyone back, and a few days before he's intubated, and I take the flight from Seattle to sit with him in the ICU. I will drive his spotless Corolla to and from the hospital every day for a week. I tell him I love him. "I wish you had asked me for help," I say to him. "You can always ask for help."

"I know. You take care of you. I'll be okay."

John Coltrane saw God in his fever-dream state of withdrawal. My dad got saved when he was a teenager, possibly out of a child's necessity to know that there is something more than living in a house with an alcoholic father that tossed him around the room like a ragdoll. And then wanting to believe there is a heaven, a place with no suffering, where he'd see his grandmother again, and every dog he ever loved. There is nothing more devastating in this life than loving someone wholeheartedly and then never seeing them again. They're just gone; that the idea of heaven is only existing in the memories of the living. It's too much to bear, isn't it?

In the interview with my dad, he's talking about how he doesn't make a lot of money, but it doesn't matter. "We went through a couple of years of just, really bad, bad, hard, hard times," he says. "And my perspective about everything changed. Now I'm happy my rent's paid and I have a car that has air conditioner in it and I'm happy as a clam about that, you know?" He smiles and laughs the hearty laugh that I miss so much.

I think I get it now.

8 NONCONFORMIST

The saxophone has existed on the margins of society since Adolphe Sax dreamed it into existence in the 1840s. It was launched to fame at the hands of disenfranchised jazz musicians, before becoming a rock n' roll symbol of seduction, or psychedelic madness—such as Dick Parry's saxophone on Pink Floyd's *Dark Side of the Moon*. While Sax may have dreamed of his instrument being used in the orchestral pit, it hasn't quite found a home there. But it *has* encouraged improvisation, experimentation, and self-expression (for better or worse).

As the saxophone became gentrified in America with the rise of the choreographed pop star, it ventured into the electronic trends of the time. The 1980s were all about synthesizers, teased hair, neon, and as we know from George Michael, the love ballad. In 1986, the year I was born, Steps Ahead released their album, *Magnetic,* featuring Michael Brecker on tenor saxophone and an Akai Electronic Wind Instrument (EWI). The EWI is an instrument that mimics a soprano but transmits its sound vocabulary through another electronic system like a synthesizer, giving its player the ability to make all manner of sounds that bring the 1980s back to us. To me, it's like the child of a saxophone and an electric guitar pumped through a twangy synthesizer. Cocteau Twins meets Coltrane. On *Magnetic,* an energetic and complex soundscape of what I imagine could be the ghost of shopping mall soundtracks past, the EWI was believed by classical composers to be the instrument of the future.[1] However, one needs to only listen to Brecker's tenor work on *Magnetic* to get a sense of relief, that the true sax solo would not be going anywhere. The EWI's popularity only lasted a few years, beyond the 1990s it makes occasional appearances in music that does not sound like "music from the future," as it was positioned upon its inception, but instead sounds nostalgic of the 1980s.

It's easy to suggest the saxophone's popularity didn't make it so far out of the 1990s, either, aside from its stronghold in the jazz world. In all its nonconformity to music and pop culture, somewhere along the way it never took off the way Adolphe Sax wanted it to. It did not fit within the symphony orchestra, it did not belong in the hands of comedy, and it survived the pop hits by the skin of its teeth, and not without permanent damage to its reputation (go ahead, ask a non-musician what they think about the saxophone. This usually

---

[1]Matthew J. Swallow. "MIDI Electronic Wind Instrument: A Study of the Instrument and Selected Works." Thesis, West Virginia University, 2016, accessed January 1, 2024, https://researchrepository.wvu.edu/cgi/viewcontent.cgi?article=7791&context=etd.

devolves into a conversation about shirtless, sexy guys. I'll wait).

The saxophone may have never landed its coveted position in the orchestral pit. But it did sneak into classical music, albeit sideways.

In 1903, Claude Debussy reluctantly wrote *Rapsodie* for the alto saxophone and an orchestra. And I mean, *reluctantly*. He ignored the commission for two years, having already been paid for the piece. The saxophone was not taken seriously in classical music. Composers wanted nothing to do with it, snubbing their noses at its sound, yet taking the money, nonetheless. Debussy finally sat down and composed the work. He wrote to a composer friend, "The saxophone is like an animal with a reed, about whose habits I know very little."[2] The fun plot twist is that his patron was a woman.

Elsie Hall, a wealthy American widow, started playing the saxophone in the mid-1890s while recovering from typhoid fever. Upon her husband's death, she founded the Orchestral Club in Boston, in the hopes of ushering amateur musicians into the world of the orchestra. She commissioned solo pieces for the saxophone and the orchestra from various notable composers. She was generations ahead of her time, especially as a woman. Especially as a woman *saxophone* player. Debussy was not amused by her, yet he did produce *Rapsodie* for her. His misogyny is palpable in his letters to his friends: "Does it not appear indecent to you, a woman

---

[2]Stephen Cottrell, *The Saxophone* (New Haven: Yale University Press, 2013), 245.

in love with the saxophone, whose lips suck at the wooden mouthpiece of this ridiculous instrument?"[3]

It appears Hall never got to perform *Rapsodie*. But her influence and tenacity in obtaining solo works for the saxophone had rippling effects on the instrument's place in classical music. Plus, I'd say she was as much of a nonconformist as Adolphe Sax, doing something she loved for the sake of an instrument that had weird ways of showing love back.

The classical composers could have been onto something, though. They recognized instantly that the saxophone is like the weird friend that you don't know how to appease or incorporate into the friend group, but you love them anyway. Musicologist Dean Winston described the saxophone's place in classical music and opera as being "strangely haunting," and its odd timbre can only be understood as some kind of "musical otherness."[4]

Hall is one of few female saxophonists that get as much attention as their male counterparts. There are many women sax players that made an impact on jazz, classical, and blues communities, that should get more attention, such as Candy Dulfer from the Netherlands (whose father was tenor jazz musician Hans Dulfer), who has performed with Pink Floyd, Beyoncé, Aretha Franklin, and other influential artists; Vi

---

[3]Ibid, 244.

[4]Winton Dean, *George Bizet: His Life and Work* (London: J.M. Dent and Sons Ltd, 1965), 03.

Redd, an iconic blues sax player who worked with Count Basie and Dizzy Gillespie, and considered a pioneer for women in blues. Chilean saxophonist Melissa Aldana was the first woman to win the Thelonious Monk International Jazz Competition in 2013. Rosa King, a tenor saxophonist from Georgia (United States) famously faced-off with Stan Getz in the 1978 Sea Jazz Festival—her success was primarily found in Europe, but her blues and funk style influenced and inspired generations of female saxophonists.

Despite the negative connotations of the sax in classical music, there are thousands of composed pieces available to saxophonists. The *Londeix Guide To The Saxophone Repertoire, 1844–2012,* for instance, is a comprehensive listing of over 29,000 works for the saxophone. That's a lot of pieces, for an instrument largely shunned.

It may not fit the bill. It might sit on the margins, disrupt the norm, like its players. But it finds a way. And really, isn't that was Adolphe Sax wanted most of all?

9 INFLUENCER

There are dozens of famous saxophone players, if not hundreds, that have rightfully claimed their immortality in the jazz age, rock 'n' roll, and pop. But if you ask anyone old enough to press play on a cassette deck in the 1990s, when asked to name the first sax player that pops into their head, they will say one name. They'll lift their head, nod, and smirk. "You mean Kenny G?" they'll ask. They press the keys of an imaginary soprano in front of them, whipping back imaginary long, curly, luxurious hair.

Kenneth Gorelick, known commercially as Kenny G., was born in Seattle in 1956, around the time jazz players were recording some of the best music we'll ever know. Thirty years later, in 1986, he released his fourth album, the breakthrough *Duotones*, which skyrocketed him to fame as a leading instrumentalist, genre-bending his way across smooth jazz, R&B, and pop. He climbed the charts. He managed to bring the saxophone back to center stage, but the package was different. Kenny G. was a slight, thin Jewish guy with long, flowing curly hair and an easy expression. He wasn't accompanying any greasy vocalists singing about jilted lovers. He wasn't playing in New Orleans jazz clubs. He is, instead, the epitome of "easy listening," which just so happens to feature a saxophone.

Kenny G. is always met with equal parts adoration and equal parts eye-rolling. Traditional jazz musicians might not enjoy that he's had astronomical success as a soloist, yet does not conform to the traditional, robust, soulful sounds of jazz. His influences are Grover Washington, Jr., not Dexter Gordon or Charlie Parker. He's never going to lie down on stage in a pool of sweat, casting aural spirituals from his horn, transfixing an audience into euphoric ecstasy and dance moves to make your mother blush.

But can you imagine?

Kenny G.'s saxophone style is restricted, his timbre being lighter, calmer, and conveying what I will call meditation music for the masses. Is it improvisational? Not at all. Is it jazz? Not technically. The issue with his success for many is a categorical one. He is not a jazz musician, but he *is* a "smooth jazz" or "contemporary jazz" musician. The mainstream media tends to lump many genres and sub-genres into one, for the sake of sales. That said, it's also easy to be irritated by his music when you are presented with it ad nauseum (malls, hold music, your company Christmas party at the Sheraton). He enraged scores of jazz fans when he dubbed over Louis Armstrong's "What a Wonderful World" in 1999, which felt sacrilegious. But the masses loved it, and he *is* an influential artist, whether we like it or not. He's performed with Whitney Houston, Michael Bolton, Barry Manilow, and scores of other R&B artists. His saxophone acts as the successful pop star, itself. He has sold over 75-million records, and had over 1.5 billion streams, making him the most successful instrumentalist in the modern era.[1] He still tours today, and in fact—a quick search tells me he's playing five shows in his hometown of Seattle at the end of the month, a few miles from my apartment. I would never go because my father, and all my diehard jazz friends, would disown me. "Kenny G." was a four-letter word in my household. Whenever somebody compared my dad's playing to Kenny G., it was a great offense. But the dude sells records and tickets. All five Seattle shows are sold out. He's laughing all the way to the bank.

The saxophone's popularity over time has not been limited to flesh and bone; it has been a feature of television shows and movies, and not always in the best light. Rob Lowe's sleazy, bad-boy character in *St. Elmo's Fire* carries his alto around with him everywhere, like an emotional support animal, slung over his shoulder, no case in sight. Lowe's womanizing character does not age well, and it's easy to feel sorry for the poor alto as he carelessly places it on the bar top.

In the final scene of the cult classic film *The Lost Boys*, a buff and shirtless Tim Cappello plays saxophone and sings a cover of The Call's 1986 single, "I Still Believe (Great Design)" during a tense moment for the protagonist,

---

[1] "Kenny G Artist Page," Concord Music, accessed June 16, 2024, https://concord.com/artist/kenny-g/.

Michael (Jason Patric), as he makes eyes with the dancing and exuberant Star (Jami Gertz). Cappello, listed in the cast as "Beach Concert Star," covered in chains, pumps his tie-dye-clad hips and tosses his long ponytail around the air along with his saxophone as the crowd dances. Cappello is cast as the stereotypical sexy, oiled-up sax guy, furthering the concept that the saxophone had become nothing more than a cheesy gimmick. In reality, Cappello is a talented sax player who recorded and toured with Tina Turner for fifteen years. But one night of filming in Santa Cruz overshadows his career, which is both a gift and a curse for Cappello. "I did so many records with [Tina] and all this stuff? It means nothing," he said in a 2020 interview with *Gizmodo.* "I'll go to a convention or I'll go do a gig and I'll have a picture of me and her. Maybe I'll sign one or two a day. It's just all stills from *The Lost Boys*. That's what people want and that's what they see me as."

Cappello's revival to fame came along around 2010, when Saturday Night Live (who boasts the talented former Tower of Power sax player Lenny Pickett as their band director) had a digital short featuring an oily, chest-baring Jon Hamm as "Sergio," a sexy sax player that appears to Andy Samberg in the form of a terrible curse placed on him by a mysterious man (Fred Armisen). The saxophone, naturally, being used as a symbol of annoying intrusion, cliché, and piloted by a 1980s beefcake. But it didn't upset Cappello. It relaunched his career. "For the first time in my life, I'll finish a song, and it's not even 'I Still Believe,' just something for my album or something. And the roar that comes from [the audience], it like literally knocks me back," he tells *Gizmodo*. "It's the most fun that I've ever had and [it's all because of] this crazy little thing that I did. It just goes to show you, always say yes, and always bring everything that you can to the table."[2]

Around the same year as the SNL short, a social media stunt threw the saxophone back under the bus as a comedy instrument, when "Sexy Sax Man," (aka: Sergio Flores) a random guy in a mullet wig, aviator sunglasses, suspenders, and no shirt (or the alternative, a Members Only jacket), hops atop fast food tables, crashes mall food courts, and checkout lanes of grocery stores and random business conferences to blare the solo from "Careless Whisper" on a loop—that is, until he gets thrown out by security. This viral video from 2011 has over 44-million views, and more than 32,000 snarky comments.[3]

In Beth Henley's 1981 Pulitzer Prize-winning play *Crimes of the Heart,* about three sisters from the American South who struggle to cope with their traumatic lives, one sister buys a saxophone in an impulsive act, hoping it will allow her to escape her life instead of dealing with her own grief. She is not successful. Less complex characters like Lisa

---

[2]Germain Lussier, "The True Story of 'The Lost Boys' Sax Man," *Gizmodo*, April 14, 2020, accessed June 14, 2024, https://gizmodo.com/the-true-story -of-the-lost-boys-sax-man-1842774832.
[3]dikemiva, "Sexy Sax Man Careless Whisper Prank feat. Sergio Flores (directors cut)," YouTube Video, March 12, 2011, https://www.youtube.com /watch?v=GaoLU6zKaws&t=133s.

Simpson, from *The Simpsons,* has been playing the baritone (as an eight-year-old) for the better part of thirty years. Her mentor, jazz sax player "Bleeding Gums Murphy," is loosely based on Sonny Rollins, who famously took a three-year sabbatical following his rising success in 1959, to practice his saxophone craft every day on the Williamstown Bridge.[4]

For all its comedy (and animation), Lisa Simpson had a real influence on young girls in the late 1990s, creating a small-scale sax craze that caused an uptick in girls picking up the instrument.

And who could forget one of the most memorable sax players of 1990s pop culture—the scandalous 42nd President of the United States, Bill Clinton. His tenor saxophone made nearly as many waves as he did during his time in the White House. His simple "cool dude" style worked wonders as a marketing tactic during his 1992 appearance on Arsenio Hall, where he played "Heartbreak Hotel." Clinton's passable saxophone stylings helped him win the young and minority votes, and the presidential election five months later.

And if you've ever watched *Parks and Recreation,* it isn't hard to fall for Ron Swanson's secret alter-ego, Duke Silver, who plays tenor for a jazz trio. Middle-aged women croon over Silver's smooth timbre and seductive banter, each of these traits possessing Silver as he holds a sax.

---

[4]"Lisa's Saxophone," Simpsons Wiki, accessed December 14, 2023, https://simpsons.fandom.com/wiki/Lisa%27s_saxophone.

The saxophone, unlike any other instrument, has seen over a hundred years' worth of success, incrimination, misunderstanding, and often landing at the feet of laughter just as soon as it begins to recover from its last fall. The rise of the internet and social media has kept the instrument in ebbs and flows of popularity. In 2010, Sergey Igorevich Stepanov donned an 1980s-inspired outfit and played a memorable alto jingle at the Eurovision Song Contest. His band, SunStroke Project, did not win, but the clip of him gyrating on stage with his saxophone became an internet meme. Now known as "Epic Sax Guy," Stepanov has placed the saxophone into the categorical dissonance of the bait-and-switch prank, Rickrolling, instead called "Saxrolling." Vaudeville is alive and well, it just requires Wi-Fi.

Then there's social media artists that genuinely want to make people happy with the saxophone, like Jazzajilo, who posts videos playing his sax in public parks surrounded by animatronic animals dancing, a banner reading "DANCING IS HAPPINESS" posted next his tooting and bobbing horn. It may not be high art, but it's hard not to smile at a joyful man playing a saxophone next to dancing cats.

If history has taught us anything about the saxophone, it's that it is, above all else, a survivor. It's survived war, oppression, poverty, and its best players as they made way for the next generation of great players. The saxophone still has much to teach us. Today, artists like Colin Stetson are doing innovative things with the sax—his style involves altissimo (not unlike SNL's band leader, Lenny Pickett), circular breathing, multiphonics, key clicking, and . . . growling. The sound that Stetson outputs is almost otherworldly, equal part digeridoo and ancient Celtic carnyx (a terrifying horn meant to intimidate opponents during warfare). Yet somehow, it is technically enjoyable and beautiful. Stetson's meditative approach to his style is genuine, and his unique sound in high demand, having played with musicians and bands like Lou Reed, LCD Soundsystem, Tom Waits, and The National. The haunting, and downright eerie sounds produced from Stetson's baritone are also frequently called upon for horror movie soundtracks, including *Hereditary* and *Texas Chainsaw Massacre*.[5]

Other saxophonists like Rudresh Mahanthappa, an American jazz musician who blends classic improvisation with the Carnatic music of his parents' native southern India, are making modern jazz sound global, spiritual.

The saxophone is nothing if not adaptable, as unique as its players soul.

It seems like every day I read a *New York Times* obituary of a "jazz saxophone legend," from Charles Gayle, Tony Coe, Wayne Shorter, and Carlos Garnett—all whom we lost in 2023 alone. But with their passing we have modern saxophonists heralding new territory, like Chris Potter, James Carter, James Brandon Lewis, Anna Webber, and countless others—all creating unique fusions and post-bop

[5]"Bio," Colin Stetson Official Website, accessed June 16, 2024, https://www.colinstetson.com/bio.

music worth spinning on a record player. And like jazz, vinyl records have not disappeared. Modern jazz players are still pressing their albums on vinyl and CDs, and collectors have never been more eager to oblige.

I reach out to the biggest jazz fan I know, Craig Morgan Teicher, an award-winning poet and amateur musician who has been listening to jazz since he was seventeen years old, a teen of the 1990s who was looking for something to speak to his grief after losing his mom. He found he could not bear music with words, so he went to Borders and bought a handful of jazz CDs. And that's how it got him. "In addition to hearing it and feeling it, you can think about it; and that actually appreciating it requires you think about it while you feel it," he tells me over a Zoom call. "Which makes it active, and something you have to choose to participate in. It's like Pac-Man with his little dots. It's something to chew on as you go along."

The saxophone, he says, is the jazz instrument allows its player to "communicate so much humanity and personality, because it's like your breath; it's a column of you," it is a key to living. He believes that jazz is crucial in our understanding of humanity, especially as a powerful voice for the marginalized. "[Jazz] is a central artform for Black Americans during a century when they had to fight for their freedom and their legal standing in a country that is endlessly racist."

And jazz? It's hasn't been around very long, but its catalog is tremendous. Overwhelming. According to Teicher, its finite history is what makes it so enjoyable for record collectors. It is a catalog, a book, of eras. "It's one of the reasons people love vinyl. And, you know," he laughs, "you could say the whole vinyl thing is about object fetishists who want an object to fetishize. What better object than the very book of itself? These records that enact the chronological history of the music."

It reminds us that there is so much music to be uncovered in the past, but also so many new sounds and layers to look forward to.

In the season-two finale of the hit FX show, *Reservation Dogs*, the teenage protagonists finally make it to the California coast to let go of their grief for their friend, who died by suicide. It is a scene both powerful and moving as the kids celebrate life and their community on the reservation, despite their profound despair. In the final moments, they walk away from the beach as Tim Cappello revives his rendition of "I Still Believe," which brings the storyline full circle, as the teens brought up the musician earlier in the episode, their dearly departed friend (Daniel) was a fan of *The Lost Boys*. In a powerful way, the Cappello's revival is a bittersweet nostalgia to viewers, who can easily relate to the feeling of grief for those lost, as well as the need to let go; that something as simple as a song from a movie that turned the instrument into cliché can, once again, be reimagined into something meaningful to let our lost ones know we will not forget them.

The serpentine instrument that Adolphe Sax created almost two hundred years ago has made its mark on

American culture. Its influence on everyone is both relatable and yet highly personal. Its power over its player—as well as its audience—ebbs and flows as trends change, as our culture shifts, as we live and die.

The saxophone will always find its way back.

EPILOGUE

TWO HORNS

The sax possesses, it entertains, it saves. Sometimes, it damns. The more I try to ask the universe, what *is it* about this instrument? I'm met with more questions; the more I learn about the saxophone and its players, its legacy, the more I need to know.

In my closet, propped against the fancier dresses and blazers that I rarely wear, are my father's two saxophones, a Viking M60 Valkyrie tenor, and an Antigua Winds 590BLQ soprano. The Yamaha alto went back to my sister, who had first learned to play it in beginner band. Her daughter now plays it in beginner band. I tell her: keep playing. We need more female saxophonists in this world.

The two saxophones and a red, beat-up Puma shoebox full of mouthpieces and reeds, those are what I have left of my father. This is an inheritance of love. I think about getting the horns professionally cleaned. But I don't. Every time I open the cases and peek the polished brass, the soft dark velvet of the liner, my chest splits wide open, and I snap them closed, fast like jaws, like when my dad used to tell me, "Shut your mouth, or you'll catch flies!" My heart sinks with guilt because I don't know how to play them (and they are meant to be played). I will, selfishly, never sell them. My people, we are sentimental. These two horns are what connect me to the sometimes mysterious and sometimes frustrating person in my life that I loved so much.

He'd probably love this book, despite its beginner tone, with an asterisk next to all the things I got wrong, the people or key historical moments of this instrument that I glossed over or forgot to mention (I am sure, reader, there are hundreds of them). He'd be upset that Boots Randolph and Michael Brecker didn't get entire chapters to themselves. For that, especially, I am sorry.

I recently attended a lecture by a writer and illustrator I admire for his devotion to fairy tales and the immortality of objects. He talked about an object's haunting ability to outlive us all—that each one tells its own rich story. There is mighty power in an object, and in a way, we all find ourselves indebted to them. I feel that in the weight of these two saxophones, each conjuring my dad as a little boy in the sixth grade, loaded up on a bus heading to the high school to participate in band because his small school in the sticks didn't have a music program. I picture him in Kansas City in 1972, having made first chair in the National F.F.A. band. Then a year later, in Russia and London as a seventeen-year-old, playing his saxophone and laughing with his bandmates as they tasted the freedoms of adulthood and globetrotting—all because of music they made.

Music may change over the years, but we will always have it, no matter the medium. The saxophone's form hasn't changed much since its inception, suggesting that Adolphe Sax's vision for the instrument was centuries ahead of his time.

The two saxophones in my closet radiate joy, nostalgia, and everything good and bad that the instrument has given to thousands of its players and audiences over the past century. They're heavy, and some might say they carry the weight of the player's soul. And it's a hopeful feeling, something that helps me navigate the impossibility of a world without my dad in it. But now, I acknowledge that I am lucky. He never died; I have recordings and albums of him playing saxophone. There are over 1,200 posts he made on his favorite web forum, Sax on the Web, that I have yet to read. He was obsessed with researching the latest, greatest music equipment, and then finding the best (affordable) alternatives. It's all complicated, and it's like trying to decipher another language that I will never speak fluently. And again, there's the interview. Forty-five minutes of getting to listen to him talk in his Southern twang about why he started playing saxophone in the first place. There are details I know he left out, because he never talked about the more painful parts of his childhood. I get to hear him laugh, throw his head back in the way that always made me do the same, when he'd chuckle so hard, he'd start coughing and run out of breath. Some say the saddest thing about losing a loved one is that they forget their laughter or voice over time. But I get to have this—and all those saxophone recordings—forever, my dad's voice immortal. And in a way I also get to stand next to him at the grocery store whenever "Baker Street" plays on the overhead speakers, or sit next to him in the Toyota car service waiting room when Pink Floyd's "Us and Them" pumps out of the ceiling as smooth and refreshing as the cold air conditioning. He's there, right next to me, waving his finger in the air, leaning forward, his ear toward the speakers, saying, "Shh—hush, listen!" And I do.

ACKNOWLEDGEMENTS

My eternal gratitude to the editors of this series, Christopher Schaberg and Ian Bogost, and Haaris Naqvi and Hali Han at Bloomsbury for keeping me on track and ushering this thing into the world of paper. I'm sorry that you now cannot unhear the saxophone everywhere you go.

To everyone at the Bennington Writing Seminars who put up with my chaotic rants about jazz, the saxophone, my dad, and the Deep South, and offered the kindest, most generous encouragement and sound advice—thank you. Gold stars to: Jill McCorkle, Amy Hempel, Peter Trachtenberg, Stuart Nadler, Elizabeth McCracken, Edward Carey, Megan Culhane Galbraith, Mark Wunderlich, Hugh Ryan, Shawna Kay Rodenberg, Cathy Gee Graney, Katie Marya, Kerry Madden-Lunsford, Chandler Ford, Christy Ammons, Juliette Macron, Alyson Williams, James LaRowe, Guillermo Rebollo Gil, Sarah Zoric, Kelly Marages (and Judy), Ariél Martinez (and Frida), and extra stars to Dinah Lenney—who introduced me to this wonderful series. A special thank you to Craig Morgan Teicher, my favorite person to talk to about all things jazz, records, and music (and sometimes, life, but mostly dogs). Thank you for telling me how you came to jazz. Tell Cashew I said thanks, too.

To my sister, Maggie, for being my most enthusiastic cheerleader. And Jo and Sean (#Mickey), for all the good food, conversations, and laughs. I can't believe I got so lucky to know you both. Thank you for all the advice (and brownies).

Jessica Danger, thank you for talking me off the cliff and reading a draft of this book in the eleventh hour. Your keen eye is so appreciated, and I am touched by your own story of the saxophone. It works in mysterious ways.

Mark Sepinuck and 10MFAN, thank you for helping me understand the nuances of mouthpieces and how things work. Moreso, for being a good friend to my dad. We do still have the music, and isn't that wonderful?

I am grateful to everyone at the Bread Loaf community. It was lovely to work with you all *on the mountain,* especially David Treuer. Carroll Beauvais, I'm so glad I randomly sat next to you in the barn that first night with my glass of cheap wine. What would I do without you?

Can you thank entire genres of music? Too cliché? I'm doing it anyway. Thank you to jazz, pop, rock, and anyone that has ever used the saxophone as a voice when they had none. As Chuck Palahniuk would say, may one of your many, many graves always be inside my head.

To anyone I missed, I am sorry, and thank you. I owe you a coffee.

Todd and Gus, you are my biggest supporters, and I couldn't have done this without you.

Most of all, to Greg. Wherever you are, I hope you are having a large time.

Portions of the Prologue first appeared in *The Rumpus*.

INDEX

700 Club, The   63, 98–9

Adderley, Julian "Cannonball"
    36, 55
A Streetcar Named Desire   79

bankruptcy   14, 17, 21
Basie, Count   52–4, 109
bebop   3, 52–5, 59, 62, 71, 100
Bechet, Sidney   48–50
Berlioz   10–12, 21, 27
Birdland   66
Birmingham   3, 33, 36–7, 63
blackface   40
blues   48, 51, 108–9
Bostic, Earl   55
Brown Brothers, the   40
Brown, Tom   40
Brussels   10
Brussels Exhibition of
    1841   10

Cannon, Ace   34
Caldwell, Happy   51
Carafa, Michele   15

Cash, Johnny   64
Cherry Blossom   53
Chevy Lumina   35
Chicago   50, 52
Christmas   1–3, 71, 76, 100,
    112
circus   40–1
Clemons, Clarence   30
Clinton, Bill   116
C-melody saxophone   42,
    50–1
Coltrane, John   31, 40, 55, 65,
    68, 91–4, 103, 106
Covid   1–2, 71–3, 76–7, 101
Cracker Barrel   33
Crimes of the Heart   115

Dark Side of the Moon, Pink
    Floyd   34
Davis, Miles   55
Devil's Horn, The   75
Dibango, Manu   76
Donizetti, Gaetano   12,
    22–3
Don Sebastian   12–3

Emperor Napoleon III   21
Evans, Stump   51

Final Destination   13

G, Kenny   111–13
Gillespie, Dizzy   54–5, 109
Getz, Stan   30, 35, 56, 65, 68, 109
Gordon, Dexter   30, 56, 112
Great Depression, the   43, 53
Green, Johnny   52

Halevy   10
hard bop   55
Hawkins, Coleman   50–3, 65
health insurance   71
Hodges, Jonny   55
Holiday, Billie   52
Holmes, G.E.   41
Horwood, Wally   9

improvisation   47–9, 51–3, 55, 57, 105, 112, 118

Jacksonville State University   34
Jones, Jo   53–4
Journal des Debats 12

Kansas City   52–5, 124
King Louis-Phillipe I, France   14, 17

King Victor Emmanuel II, Italy   15
Konitz, Lee   76

lawsuits   19, 23
Legion of Decency, the   79
Legion of Honour, the   21
Logan, Giuseppe   76
Lost Boys, The   113–14, 120
    Capello, Tim ("Beach Concert Star")   113–14

Mamie Smith's Original Jazz Hounds   51
Marching Southerners, The   35
Master Saxophone Sextet, the   42
Meyerbeer   10
Mississippi River   47
Monk, Thelonius   54, 109
Monroe, Marilyn   79
Morton, Jelly Roll   48
mouthpieces   28–31, 37, 123
Musical Spillers, the   40
Muzak   74

National Endowment for the Arts (NEA)   67
Nazi Germany   80

ophicleide   11, 25

Paris   10, 12, 15, 19–23, 49
Parker, Charlie   54–6, 65–6, 112
Parks and Recreation   116
 Swanson, Ron (Duke Silver)   116
Pell City, Alabama   33–5, 37, 63
Peralta, Marcelo   76
Presley, Elvis   64
Pulitzer Prize   56, 115

Queen Marie-Amelie, France   14
QVC   37

racism   40, 47
ragtime   41, 48, 51
Randolph, Boots   34, 124
Robertson, Prince   51
Rollins, Sonny   116
Royal School of Singing   9

Sacramento, California   1, 37, 71, 74
Saturday Night Live   114–15, 117
 Lenny Pickett, band director   114, 117
Sax, Adolphe-Edouard   22–3
Sax, Antoine-Joseph (Adolphe)   7–11, 14, 23–5, 27,

40–2, 56, 65, 68, 105–6, 108-9, 120, 125
Selmer   23, 27, 29, 37
Sepinuck, Mark   28–31
Simpsons, The   116
 Simpson, Lisa   116
Six Brown Brothers, The   39
Smith, Clay   41
Smith, Elliott   94
Soviet Union   80
Springsteen, Bruce   30
Stetson, Colin   117–18
Storyville, New Orleans   41, 47–8, 53
suicide   14, 20, 66, 94, 120

Tin Pin Alley   48
T.J. Maxx   33
Twin Peaks   33

United States Collegiate Wind Band   34

Vallée, Rudy   44
vaudeville   39, 40–1, 55, 64, 117

White, E.B.   39
Wiedoeft, Rudy   42, 44, 65
Woods, Phil   55, 81

Young, Lester   54